Economics of Fisheries in North East India

About the Author

Kaju Nath, Ph.D. got his Doctoral Degree from Rajiv Gandhi University (A Central University), Rono Hills, Itanagar, Arunachal Pradesh. At present he is working as an Assistant Professor in Economics, Department of Humanities and Social Sciences, National Institute of Technology Agartala, Tripura. Earlier to the present assignment he worked in five major research projects sponsored by Finance Commission, Planning Commission, Indian Council of Social Science Research (ICSSR), etc. He was also a Visiting Faculty for MBA in the Department of Management, Rajiv Gandhi University and Resource Person for BA (Distance Education) in the same University. He presented a number of papers in international and national seminars, conferences, etc. A number of published research papers in reputed journals and edited books are to his credit.

Economics of Fisheries in North East India

Opportunities and Challenges

Kaju Nath

CONCEPT PUBLISHING COMPANY PVT. LTD.
NEW DELHI-110059

ISBN-13 : 978-93-5125-150-7

First Published 2016

Published and Printed by

Concept Publishing Company Pvt. Ltd.
A/15-16, Commercial Block, Mohan Garden
New Delhi-110059 (India)
T: 25351460, 25351794, *F*: 091-11-25357109
E: publishing@conceptpub.com, W: www.conceptpub.com
Editorial Office: H-13, Bali Nagar, New Delhi-110 015, India.

Cataloging in Publication Data--*Courtesy:* D.K. Agencies (P) Ltd. <docinfo@dkagencies.com>

Nath, Kaju, author.
Economics of fisheries in North East India : opportunities and challenges / Kaju Nath.
pages cm
Originally presented as the author's thesis (Doctoral--Rajiv Gandhi University).
Includes bibliographical references.
ISBN 9789351251507

1. Fisheries--Economic aspects--India--Arunāchal Pradesh. I. Title.

H300.A78N38 2016 DDC 338.37270954163 23

Dedicated
to

My Respected Teachers
Loving Mother
Shilpi Nath
Sweet Sister
Bornali Nath
&
Dear Friends

Foreword

I am happy to present and introduce this book on 'Economics of Fisheries in North East India — Opportunities and Challenges' by Kaju Nath. The book is an outcome of his Doctoral Research work who for the first time worked on economics of fisheries in Arunachal Pradesh.

There has been a growing reorganization of the vast growth potential of fish in India mainly from inland water bodies and thereby providing much needed edible protection and augmenting the income of rural poor. India has abundant natural endowment, conventional wisdom and human skills in respect of intensified fish farming. As a result, India has the distinction of being one of the largest producers of fish in the world and ranks second in terms of inland fish production after China. However, India has not utilized its full potential of fish production. For example, the North Eastern Region of India has vast untapped potential for diverse aquatic resources in terms of many rivers, streams, floodplain wetlands, lakes, ponds and large area under rice-fish culture system. This water resource harbours 258 fish species belonging to 21 families and 76 genera. Among these some species are known for sports; a few for their potential ornamental value and some other as food fish including a few highly priced exotic fishes. These valuable resources need to be harnessed properly to earn sustainable return. Hence, there is need of study regarding the production, resource use efficiency and marketing structure of inland fisheries in the region which has a large potential for upliftment of economic condition of poor people.

Kaju Nath has responded to the call of time by understanding the present valuable study in respect of Arunachal Pradesh. It is the largest State in terms of area and the richest State in terms of aquatic resources among the States of North Eastern Region of India. In this study attempts have been made to examine the productivity, factors of variation in productivity, resource use efficiency in fish production as well as marketing structure of fishes in Arunachal Pradesh. The researcher also attempts to identify the factors that impede the development of fisheries in the State. Efforts are also made to evaluate the role of Government programme towards the development of inland fisheries sector. The study is based on the data collected from selected fish farmers from different villages in selected agro-climatic zones of Arunachal Pradesh. The main policy emanate from the study are encouragement of public private partnership, introduction of microcredit among fish farmers and integrated approach of fishery along with agriculture and other allied activities. If these policy suggestions coupled with other lesson learnt from the country are implemented, Arunachal Pradesh can become one of the largest producers of fish in the region.

The book will have different relevance to the policy makers in the Ministry of Agriculture and Fisheries as well as to the other Government agencies. I can say that the book will contribute to the growing body of literature in the area of economics of fisheries as a whole and North Eastern region of India in particular.

(Prof. Amitava Mitra)
Professor
Department of Economics
Former Head of Department
Former Dean, Faculty of Social Sciences

Acknowledgements

I am indebted to many institutions and people who helped me from the inception to the completion of the work in different ways. The main task of turning this work into academic reality lies with one of my revered teachers and guide, Prof. Amitava Mitra, (Professor, Department of Economics, Rajiv Gandhi University) for showing such interest in my work and progress, for guiding me and for pushing me to do the best I ever could, from the very beginning to the very end in spite of his busy schedule. Any word of gratitude, on my part will always fall short of his effortless contribution.

I am grateful to Prof. N.C. Roy, Prof. S. K. Nayak, Dr. (Ms.) V. Upadhyay, Dr. L. Nochi, Dr. M. Lama and other faculty members of the Department of Economics, Rajiv Gandhi University for their continuous encouragement and advice. I am also grateful to Dr. Debasis Neogi (National Institute of Technology Agartala); Prof. Sib Ranjan Misra (Visva-Bharati University, Santiniketan); Prof. D. N. Das (Department of Zoology, Rajiv Gandhi University); Dr. Brojen Das (Indira Gandhi Government College, Tezu), for their cooperation and suggestions in various ways during various stages of my research work.

I am thankful to staffs of Rajiv Gandhi University Library. Acknowledgement also goes to Staffs of Tata Institute of Social Science Library, Mumbai; Calcutta University Library, Kolkata; ICSSR-NERC Library, Shillong; NEHU Library, Shillong; NEC Library, Shillong; ICAR Library, Barapani, Shillong; Research Library, Itanagar; State Library, Itanagar; Arunachal Pradesh State Assembly Library, Naharlagun.

I acknowledge Indian Council of Social Science Research, North Eastern Regional Centre, Shillong and Indian Statistical Institute, Kolkata for providing training on Statistical Package for Social Sciences (SPSS) and other relevant statistical software without which mathematical treatment of the data during the research work would be difficult and time consuming task.

Very special thanks go to Mitra Madam (Associate Professor (Retd.), D.N. Government College, Itanagar) for her cooperation, caring and endless encouragement during the research work.

During the course of field work, I received invaluable help from Amung, Bhovendra Kumar Mishra (Bobhy) and Racho Rina who accompanied and helped me in the collection of field data. I am thankful to them for their support, cooperation and hospitality. Thanks goes to the surveyed fish farmers, especially to the educated youths, for their valuable time and cooperation, who helped me from different angles during the field survey.

I also take this opportunity to express my gratefulness to Dani Yabo, Rajesh Gurung, Mrinal Debnath, Sandeep Rai, Aloya Linggi, Dujum Lomi, Karmar Basar, Rupan Mazumdar, Mithi Perme, Tashi Tsomu, N. Appu Raza, Nokgen Wangsu, Khoda Sumphi, Fames Linggi, Tagam Dabi, Ajit Debnath, Biman Kr. Nath and many more faceless names and nameless faces for their constant encouragement throughout my academic career and during the research work.

There are people, other than those mentioned above who have helped me in more than one ways to pursue the research work. Their timely help and sacrifices meant a lot to me. In this regard, Smt. Shilpi Nath (my mother) and Miss Bornali Nath (my younger sister) both have been the silent source of inspiration and deserve special accolade since they had to bear maximum burnt and pain in my absence and inactivity. My thanks also go to other members of my family for their encouragement through the course of this study.

(Kaju Nath)

Assistant Professor

Department of Humanities and Social Sciences

National Institute of Technology Agartala

Tripura-799 055

Contents

Foreword	*(vii)*
Acknowledgements	*(ix)*
List of Tables	*(xi)*
List of Figures	*(xviii)*
List of Maps	*(xviii)*
Glossary	*(xix)*
Abbreviations	*(xxiii)*
1. Introduction	**1-13**
Background of the Study	1
Objectives of the Study	4
Research Questions	5
Data Base and Methodology of the Study	5
Analytical Framework	8
Limitations of the Study	11
Chapter Organisation	12
2. Productivity, Resource Use Efficiency, Livelihood Options and Marketing Structure in Fisheries: An Overview of Literatures	**14-36**
Introduction	14
Production and Productivity in Fishery	15
Resource Use Efficiency in Fishery	19
Livelihood Options in Fishery	21
Marketing Structure in Fishery	24
Other Important Studies	26
Studies in North Eastern Region of India and Arunachal Pradesh	29

3. Fisheries in India, North Eastern Region of India and Arunachal Pradesh **37-58**

Introduction 37

Fisheries in India 38

Fisheries in the North Eastern Region of India 44

Status of Fisheries in Arunachal Pradesh 50

Trends of Production of Fishes in Arunachal Pradesh 53

4. Socio-economic Characteristics, Livelihood Linkages of Surveyed Fish Farmers and Operational Features of Sampled Ponds **59-78**

Introduction 59

Brief Description of Surveyed Districts 59

Socio-economic Characteristics of Fish Farmers Surveyed 66

Occupational Structure of Surveyed Fish Farmers 70

Livelihood Linkages of the Fish Farmer Surveyed 72

Operational Features of the Sampled Ponds 75

5. Productivity, Resource Use Efficiency and Marketing Structure (A Quantitative Analysis) **79-95**

Introduction 79

Productivity Analysis of Surveyed Fish Ponds 79

Results and Interpretation of Regression Analysis 82

Cost Benefit Analysis 86

Resource Use Efficiency 89

Marketing Structure in the Surveyed Districts 92

Marketing Efficiency in the Study Area 93

6. Constraints for Adoption of Fish Farming and Evaluation of Government Policies regarding Fisheries **96-112**

Introduction 96

Constraints faced by the Surveyed Fish Farmers 96

Role of Government in Fishery Development 103

Central Sector Schemes and Centrally Sponsored Schemes in the Fishery Sector 107

Achievements of Fish Farmers Development Agency in Arunachal Pradesh 110

7. Principal Findings and Policy Implications 113-131

Introduction 113

Principal Findings 113

Policy Implications 128

Appendix **132-146**

I (A) Major Fish Producing Countries of World, 2004 132

I (B) Major Inland Fish Producing Countries of World, 2004 132

II Composition of Fish Production in India during 1990-91 to 2010-11 133

III (A) Per Capita Consumption of Fish in North Eastern Region of India, 2009-10 134

III (B) Per Capita Consumption of Fish in Arunachal Pradesh during 1993-94 to 2009-10 134

IV Composition of Revenue and Capital Expenditure in Fishery Sector by Central Government during 1997-98 to 2009-10 135

V Production and Requirement of Fish in North Eastern States of India in 2010-2011 136

VI Questionnaire 137

Bibliography **147-163**

Index **164**

List of Tables

3.1	Inland Water Resources of India	39
3.2	Marine Fishery Resources of India	39
3.3	Fish Production in World and India during 1950 to 2004	41
3.4	Production and Growth Rate of Major Agricultural Commodities and Fisheries in India during 1949-50 to 1998-99	43
3.5	Contribution of Fishery Sector to India's GDP and Agricultural Sector during 1970-71 to 2010-11	43
3.6	Inland Water Resources of North Eastern Region of India	44
3.7	Fish Production in North Eastern Region of India during 1990-91 to 2010-11	46
3.8 (A)	Contribution of Fisheries to Agriculture and Allied Activities and NSDP in North Eastern Region of India during 2004-05 to 2010-11	47
3.8 (B)	Contribution of Fisheries to Agriculture and Allied Activities and NSDP in North Eastern Region of India during 2004-05 to 2010-11	49
3.9	Inland Water Resources of Arunachal Pradesh	50
3.10	Developed Paddy-*cum*-Fish Culture Area and Total Fish Culture Area in Arunachal Pradesh	51
3.11	Utilization Status of Fishery Resources of Arunachal Pradesh, 2004	52
3.12	Area under Paddy-*cum*-Fish Culture and Production of Fish in Arunachal Pradesh during 1997-98 to 2010-11	55

3.13 Contribution of Fishery Sector to the Agriculture and Allied Activities and Total NSDP of Arunachal Pradesh during 1981-82 to 2011-12 56
4.1 Socio-economic Data of Lohit District 62
4.2 Socio-economic Data of Lower Subansiri District 64
4.3 Fish Farmer's Household Surveyed as per District, Block and Village 65
4.4 Age-wise Distribution of Fish Farmers in the Surveyed Districts 66
4.5 Educational Status of Fish Farmer Surveyed 67
4.6 Family Size of Fish Farmers Surveyed 68
4.7 Gender-wise Distribution of Fish Farmers Surveyed 68
4.8 Gender's Roles in Fish Farming Activities among Surveyed Fish Farmers Household 70
4.9 Average Working Hours by Surveyed Fish Farmers per Day during the Fishing Seasons 71
4.10 Occupational Structure of Fish Farmers Surveyed 71
4.11 Experience in Fishing Related Activities of Fish Farmers Surveyed 72
4.12 Distribution of Households on the basis of Major Livelihood Strategies in the Surveyed Areas 73
4.13 Distribution of Share of Income from Different Sources under various Livelihood Combinations in the Surveyed Districts 74
4.14 Combinations of Major Source of Collection of Fish Seeds 77
4.15 Size Class Distribution of the Numbers and Area of Currently Operated Water Units 77
5.1 Distribution of Productivity by Size of Pond 80
5.2 Distribution of Productivity by Number of Owners of Pond 81
5.3 Distribution of Cost and Return Analysis for Fish Production in the Study Area 87
5.4 Distribution of Profitability Estimates for Fish Production in the Study Area 88
5.5 Production Elasticities and Marginal Value Products of Various Inputs 90

5.6	Disposal of Fish through Different Marketing Channels	92
5.7	Marketing Cost, Margin and Prices in the Study Area	93
5.8	Estimates of Marketing Efficiency in Different Marketing Channels	94
6.1	Major Constraints reported in Lohit District	98
6.2	Major Constraints reported in Lower Subansiri District	98
6.3	Non-availability of Adequate Financial Assistance	100
6.4	Problem of Poaching	100
6.5	Inefficient Marketing Structure	101
6.6	Poor and Inadequate Supply of Fish Seeds	102
6.7	High Cost and Adulteration of Fish Feed	103
6.8	Financial Allocation to the Fishery Sector of Arunachal Pradesh during Various Plan Periods	104
6.9	Expenditure of State Government during 1991-92 to 2009-10	104
6.10	Composition of Revenue Expenditure and Capital Expenditure to the Total Expenditure in Fishery by State Government during 1991-92 to 2009-10	105
6.11	Fishery Infrastructure in the State of Arunachal Pradesh during 2004-05 to 2010-11	106
6.12	Central Sector Schemes and Centrally Sponsored Schemes for Fisheries in Arunachal Pradesh during Tenth and Eleventh Five Year Plans	108
6.13	Achievements of Fish Farmers Development Agencies in North Eastern Region of India till 2005-06	111

List of Figures and Maps

Figures

1.1	Design of Sample Survey	8
3.1	Fish Production in India during 1950-51 to 2010-11	39
3.2	India's Share in World Fish Production during 1980 to 2004	42
3.3	Utilization Status of Fishery Resources of Arunachal Pradesh, 2004	52
3.4	Fish Production in Arunachal Pradesh during 1990-91 to 2010-11	54
3.5	District-wise Composition of Fish Production in Arunachal Pradesh, 2009	56
4.1	Distribution of Ownership of Ponds	75
4.2	Use of Water Units other than Fishery Activities	76
6.1	Allocation in Central Sector Schemes and Centrally Sponsored Schemes for Fisheries among different States of North Eastern Region of India during Eleventh Five Year Plan	109
6.2	Functions of Fish Farmers Development Agency (FFDA)	111

Maps

1.1	Location Map of Arunachal Pradesh showing the Surveyed Districts	6
1.2	Map showing Different Agro-climatic Zones of Arunachal Pradesh	7
4.1	Location Map of Lohit District showing the Surveyed Area	60
4.2	Location Map of Lower Subansiri District showing the Surveyed Area	63

Glossary

Beel: A beel or a bheel is a term for a pond (*wetland*) with static water (as opposed to moving water in rivers and canals — typically called *khaals*), in the *Ganges - Brahmaputra flood plains* of the Eastern Indian States of West Bengal, and Assam and in the country of Bangladesh. The term owes its origins to the word of the same pronunciation meaning "pond" in the Bengali and Assamese languages.

Capture Fishery: In this kind of fishery, one does not have to sow the fish seeds. Nature is doing the job for sowing. The wild untended stock of organisms is harvested with little human interventions on either habitat variables or the biotic communities.

Cooperative: It is an autonomous association of persons who *voluntarily* cooperate for their mutual, social, economic, and cultural benefit.

Co-management: A valuable tool for the sustainable management in fisheries. It can also help in resolution of potential conflicts among user groups. As part of co-management, effective dialogue between local and tourism communities is needed, as it is a commitment on the part of non-resident stakeholders.

Culture Fisheries: In culture fisheries, the whole operation is based on captive stock with a high degree of effective human control over the physio-chemical water quality and other habitat variable. One has to sow the seeds, nurse it and tend it to the proper size before harvesting. Intensive aquaculture of fish and prawn in a pond is a typical example of culture fisheries.

Fingerling: It refers to a fish that has reached the stage where the fins can be extended and where scales have started developing throughout the body. At this stage, the fish is typically about the size of a finger.

Fish Farmers' Development Agencies: The FFDAs are registered societies, envisaging leasing of tanks and ponds owned by government and local bodies to the fish farmers on long term lease, training of farmers, supply of inputs required, and provision of financial assistance in the form of subsidy for fish pond improvement and inputs. In addition, the extension services were provided to the fish farmers to spread the technology.

Fishery: One or more stocks or species of fish or aquatic life (usually fresh water) that can be treated as a unit for conservation/management purposes.

Freshwater: Water having a low mineral content acceptable for portable purposes (< 1000 mg /litre of dissolved solid).

Habitat: The place or type of site where a biological community naturally occurs.

Hatchery: A fish hatchery is a "place for artificial breeding, hatching and rearing through the early life stages of animals, finfish and shellfish in particular". Hatcheries produce *larval* and *juvenile fish* (and shellfish and crustaceans) primarily to support the aquaculture industry where they are transferred to on-growing systems, i.e., fish farms to reach harvest size.

Inland Fisheries: Any activities conducted to extract fish and other aquatic organism from inland waters.

Microcredit: Microcredit is the extension of very small *loans* (microloans) to impoverished borrowers who typically lack *collateral*, steady employment and a verifiable *credit history*. It is designed not only to support entrepreneurship and alleviate poverty, but also in many cases to empower women and uplift entire communities by extension.

Nursery pond: This type of pond is used for nursing 2.5 to 7.5 cm fry until the desired size of fish is reached.

Public–Private Partnership: Public–Private Partnership (PPP) describes a government service or private business venture which is funded and operated through a partnership of government and one or more *private sector* companies. These schemes are sometimes referred to as PPP, P3 or P^3

Reservoir: A natural or artificial, usually open, impoundment or body of water to be used for recreation, power, flood control or drinking purposes is stored.

Self-Help Group (SHG): A self-help group (SHG) is a village-based financial intermediary usually composed of 10–20 local women. Members make small regular savings contributions over a few months until there is enough capital in the group to begin lending.

Sustainable Development (SD): SD is a requirement to the present generation to manage the resource base such that average quality of life we ensure ourselves should potentially be shared by other future generations.

Tadpole: A tadpole (also called pollywog or porwigle) is the *larval stage* in the life cycle of an *amphibian*, particularly that of a *frog* or *toad*.

Wetland: Permanently or intermittently wet areas, shallow water and land water margins that support a natural ecosystem of plants and animals that are adapted to wet conditions.

Abbreviations

A	:	Agriculture
AH	:	Animal Husbandry
AP	:	Arunachal Pradesh
AS	:	Assam
B	:	Business
BCR	:	Benefit Cost Ratio
BFDA	:	Brackish Water Fish Farmers Development Agency
CA	:	Coldwater Aquaculture
DFA	:	Development of Freshwater Aquaculture
ESR	:	Expense Structure Ratio
F	:	Fishery
FAO	:	Food and Agriculture Organisation of the United Nations
FC	:	Fixed Cost
FE	:	Fishery Extension
FFDA	:	Fish Farmers Development Agency
FFDAs	:	Fish Farmers Development Agencies
Fo	:	Forestry
FWS	:	Fishermen Welfare Schemes
GDP	:	Gross Domestic Product
GM	:	Gross Margin
GS	:	Government Supply
H	:	Horticulture
ha	:	Hectare
km	:	Kilometre
ML	:	Meghalaya

MN	:	Manipur
MS	:	Market Source
MVP	:	Marginal Value Product
MVPs	:	Marginal Value Products
MZ	:	Mizoram
NA	:	Not Available
NDDP	:	Net District Domestic Product
NEDFi	:	North Eastern Development Finance Corporation Ltd.
NER	:	North Eastern Region of India
NL	:	Nagaland
NR	:	Net Return
NSDP	:	Net State Domestic Product
OP	:	Own Pond
PHI	:	Post-Harvest Infrastructure
RCR	:	Resource Cost Ratio
RoR	:	Rate of Return
S	:	Services
SDIN	:	Strengthening of Database Information and Networking
SK	:	Sikkim
SLA	:	Sustainable Livelihood Approach
SSF	:	Small Scale Fisheries
TC	:	Total Cost
TR	:	Total Revenue
TR	:	Tripura
VC	:	Variable Cost
WTO	:	World Trade Organisation

Chapter -1

Introduction

Background of the Study

Agriculture is the main source of livelihood for the majority of the people of India despite concerted industrialization in the last six decades. Although great development took place in the field of agriculture in the form of green revolution during the last few decades in the country but, it was limited to a few areas and to a few crops only. In fact, a majority of the farmers of India are still following traditional practices of farming which not are at all remunerative. Agricultural production is hardly sufficient to meet the domestic requirements for even a period of four to five months. As a result, a majority of the farmers and rural population experienced a relative decline in their economic position and deterioration in their living standards. Therefore, there is a need for diversification of agriculture and herein lies the importance of agricultural allied activities like fishery in the rural areas of India. In fact, fishery, as a capable means of livelihood enhancement and diversification in India, has been debated since the early 1990s. However, these developments took place in a policy vacuum as most of the Departments of Fisheries were still mandated and oriented to their revenue generation, regulatory and conservation roles as against the need for using the natural resources for rural development.

Things began to change for the better since late 1990s. The increasing demand for fish and fish products domestically and in the international market, stagnating marine fish production with its associated crises and above all, availability of underutilized and unutilized water resources in inland region have forced policy makers to come out in certain interventions in the form of promotional and segmental policies. In recent years, there has been increasing realization among planners and policy-makers that aquaculture has adequate potential to provide employment and reduce poverty by creating sustainable fishery based livelihood. As a result, there is a rapid growth of fish production in India which is mainly due to increasing contribution from inland fisheries and aquaculture. Thus, with third position in total fish production and second in inland fish production (Appendix-I), India has high potential in this sector for diversification of rural economy, domestic nutritional security, income and employment generation as well as export earnings. Fisheries, now recognized, as a sunrise sector in India recorded faster growth than any of the other agricultural and allied sectors during the last few decades (Government of India, 2006). This rise in fish production was possible due to a quantum jump in inland fish production especially pond culture which is now growing at an average annual growth rate of around 13.87 per cent (Government of India, 2006).

Fishery is one of the main sources of livelihood for the rural population. However, fishery-related livelihoods are complex, dynamic and adaptive in nature (Misra, 2012). Some fisheries are engaged in fishing fulltime i.e., all year round but more commonly people fish on a part time basis. They may take advantage of seasonally available riverine and other inland resources or they may fish part time all through the year. This leaves time to engage in other activities such as farming and rearing livestock. Fishery often shows this high degree of integration with other economic activities at the local level such as agriculture trading and the provision of labour. It should be noted that fish stocks fluctuate seasonally from abundance to almost zero depending on high and low fishing seasons. During the high season, the cash income generated from selling fish can be used to invest in other assets such as livelihood diversification, which can further reduce vulnerability to poverty. There are many studies which showed that households involved in fisheries had higher income than non-fishing households in the same village or districts (Misra, 2012).

Keeping this in view, the present study has made an attempt to examine how fisheries in Arunachal Pradesh can play an important role in uplifting the economic condition of the people of the State by providing an additional source of income and employment opportunities. Arunachal Pradesh, the proposed study area is located in the extreme north eastern corner of India. The State is well endowed for inland water fisheries. For example, the State consists of around 31.94 per cent of total area of North Eastern Region of India but it contains 26.42 per cent of flood plain lakes and derelict water, 74.39 per cent of tanks and ponds as well as 56.48 per cent of total water bodies of the region (Government of India, 2012). In addition, rice-fish cultivation is an important component of fisheries in general and cultural fisheries in particular of the State. The best example of rice-fish culture of the State is the Apatani plateau of Lower Subansiri district. Thus, the State has enormous potential for development of fisheries in the region. In fact, fish from time immemorial has been an important dietary food of the people of the State. Earlier, the fishery practice in Arunachal Pradesh was predominantly captured fishing i.e., direct fishing from the wild. People in general used to exploit whatever species was available in the drainage systems, as their food resources (Das, Sarma and Mahanta, 2010). The water bodies, as well as fishing resources, were owned by community and clan. There was no restriction on individual fishing of a particular community or a clan for the consumption purpose (Choudhary *et al.*, 2008). However, sometimes huge catches of fish were done by community during festival or recreational purpose from the water bodies owned by the community. This was the common practice a few decades ago when Arunachal's economy was basically a mono-economy characterized by subsistence agriculture and a few cottage industries (Mitra, 2005). So, in traditional production system in Arunachal Pradesh, the use of capital was insignificant and the length of production was, in general, small. This involved a small waiting compared with that in production for the market. For example, catching fish in a river does not involve much waiting but a person rearing fish in a pond must wait a number of months. However, there was a gradual transformation of Arunachal economy and bartering tended to be replaced by the monetized transactions, facilitating the integration of the communal economies into a national economy. The extension of permanent cultivation along with technological changes led to the wide individualization of cultivable land. With the individualization of agricultural land, there is growing tendency of individual ownership of water bodies. In fact, in many districts of the State, most of the ponds, tanks and beels are owned by individuals. For example, fish ponds and farms owned by the people consisted of around 9200.00 hectares, as against the Government fish farms of 35.69 hectares in 2010-11 (Government of Arunachal Pradesh, 2011). Many owners of these water bodies hold the potential to catch the ornamental as well as commercial market (both domestic and international) if their culture methods are developed (Das, 2005). So, it is high time to examine the productivity of fisheries, resource use efficiency as well as the marketing structure of the fisheries of Arunachal Pradesh. However, no study on economics of fishery in this direction is done till today in the State. Hence, the present study is an attempt to fill this gap in knowledge.

Objectives of the Study

The following objectives were framed for the study :

1. To identify the opportunities of development of fisheries in the State.
2. To study the socio-economic condition of the people associated with fish farming activity in the study area and to identify various operational and structural features of ponds under which production is carried on.
3. To examine the relationship between the pond size and yield rate.
4. To analyse the relationship between output and various inputs used in sampled ponds.
5. To examine the profitability of fish farming in the study area.
6. To study the marketing structure of inland fisheries in the study area.
7. To identify the major challenges of the promotion of fisheries in the study area and to suggest suitable policy prescription.

Research Questions

As the study is explanatory in nature, the following research questions are framed in lieu of hypothesis :

1. What are the trends and growth of production of fisheries in Arunachal Pradesh since nineties?
2. What are the socio-economic characteristics as well as percentage share of fisheries to total income of rural household under various livelihood combinations of the surveyed fish farmers in the surveyed area?
3. Is there any relationship between pond size and yield rate?
4. What are the variables which affect significantly the productivity of fish in the study area?
5. What is the nature of relationship between production of fish and different inputs used?
6. What is the estimated cost and return from fish farms in the study area?
7. Does the marketing of fish work efficiently in the study area?
8. What are the major constraints faced by the fish farmers and what corrective measures could be taken to impart dynamism and vitality to this important segment of the rural economy?

Data Base and Methodology of the Study

The present study is empirical in nature. The study used both primary and secondary data. The collection of primary data was based on multistage sampling technique.

The different stages under the technique are as follows:

Stage I: Selection of districts

Stage II: Selection of blocks

Stage III: Selection of villages

Stage IV: Selection of fish farmer's household

In the first stage two districts namely Lohit and Lower Subansiri were selected by purposive sampling since almost 20 per cent of the total fish produced in Arunachal Pradesh comes from these two districts. In fact, Lohit is the largest producer of fish in the State and Lower Subansiri district is one of the largest producers of fish among the hilly districts of Arunachal Pradesh. Further, the *Apatani* plateau of Lower Subansiri district is a unique example of the paddy-cum-fish culture of the State.

In order to have a clear picture of the study area, a location map of Lohit and Lower Subansiri districts of Arunachal Pradesh is shown in Map 1.1.

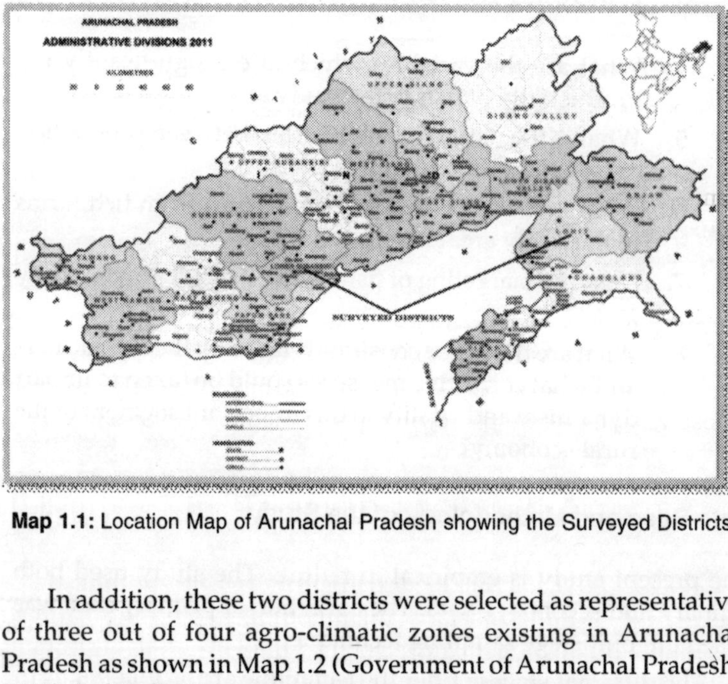

Map 1.1: Location Map of Arunachal Pradesh showing the Surveyed Districts

In addition, these two districts were selected as representative of three out of four agro-climatic zones existing in Arunachal Pradesh as shown in Map 1.2 (Government of Arunachal Pradesh, 2012). Lohit district represented tropical zone (0-900 metres) and Lower Subansiri district represented sub-tropical zone (901-1800 metres) and temperate zone (1801-3500 metres).

In the second stage, three blocks namely Tezu, Namsai-Chongkham and Lekhang from Lohit district and one block, i.e., Ziro-I from Lower Subansiri district were selected by purposive

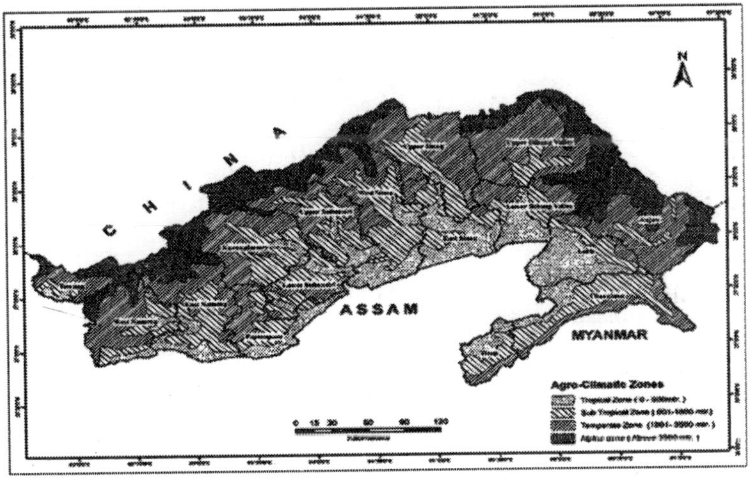

Map 1.2 : Map showing Different Agro-climatic Zones of Arunachal Pradesh

sampling on the basis of extent of fish cultivation. In the third stage, four villages from Tezu block, seven villages from Namsai-Chongkham block, three villages from Lekhang block and six villages from Ziro-I block were selected purposively where fish farming was carried on a large scale. In the final stage, the fish farmers were selected randomly. The unit of observation is the fish farmer's household. Twenty fish farmer were selected from those villages where fish farming is carried out comparatively in large scale and ten fish farmer household were selected from those villages were fish farming is done comparatively in small scale.

The details are shown in the following chart (Figure 1.1). (Next Page)

The secondary data were collected from various published and unpublished sources. The State and district level information were collected from Government offices like, Directorate of Fisheries, Government of Arunachal Pradesh, District Fishery Development Offices of Lohit and Lower Subansiri Districts, Directorate of Economics and Statistics, Government of Arunachal Pradesh, Department of Planning, Government of Arunachal Pradesh, various Government websites, etc. For National and international level data various publications and websites of Department of Animal Husbandry, Dairying and Fisheries,

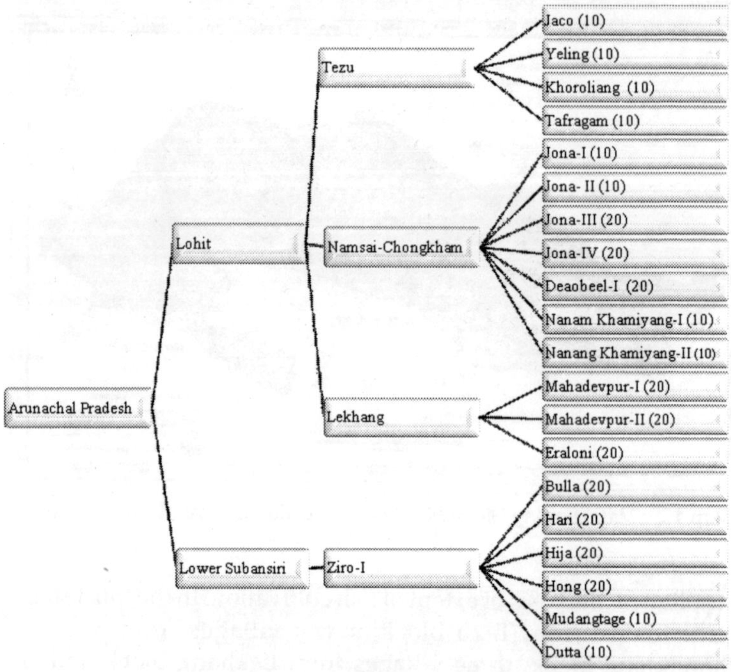

Fig. 1.1: Design of Sample Survey

(State Districts Blocks Villages/Locality)

Note: Figures in the parentheses indicate number of surveyed fish farmer households.

Ministry of Agriculture, Government of India, Census of India, Government of India, Fisheries and Aquaculture Department, Food and Agriculture Organisation of the United Nations, etc., were used. In addition information was collected from relevant books and journals, various Government policy documents, report of various committees and publications of various organizations. Several officials of relevant departments were contacted and consulted for cross examining the information and for supplementing the data required for the present study.

Analytical Framework

The log linear regression model was used to study the effect of different variables like socio-economic characteristics, cost of production, infrastructural facilities, etc. in the productivity of fish in the sampled ponds of the study area. The following model was used:

$$In\, Y = \alpha + \sum_{i=1}^{n} \beta_i X_i + U_t$$

where;

Y = productivity of fish;

α = Intercept or Constant;

X_i = Input variables (i = 1, 2...n);

β_i = Regression coefficient of ith variable; and

U_t = Error term *(assumed to have a zero mean and constant variance).*

The cost benefit analysis and profitability estimates were used to examine the cost and return of fish farming in the study area, which were given as follows:

Net Return (NR) = Total Revenue (TR) – Total Cost (TC)

Gross Margin (GM) = Total Revenue (TR) – Variable Cost (VC)

$$\text{Benefit Cost Ration} = \frac{\text{Total Reven ue (TR)}}{\text{Total Cost (TC)}}$$

$$\text{Expense Structure Ratio} = \frac{\text{Fixed Cost (FC)}}{\text{Variable Cost (VC)}}$$

$$\text{Rate of Return (RoR)} = \frac{\text{Net Return (NR)}}{\text{Total Cost (TC)}}$$

In order to study the association between output and various inputs used, Cobb-Douglas production function was used. The following model of Cobb-Douglas production function was used:

$$Y = \alpha X_i^{\beta_i} u_t$$

where;

Y = Value of gross fish production;

α = Intercept or Constant;

X_i = Input variables (i = 1, 2...n);

β_i = Regression coefficient of ith variable; and

u_t = Error term *(assumed to have a zero mean and constant variance).*

To examine the productivity of different inputs used in the production function, marginal value productivities (MVPs) of inputs were estimated by the following formula:

$$MVPx_i = \frac{\partial Y}{\partial X_i}$$

$$= \beta_i \frac{\overline{Y}}{\overline{X}_i}$$

where;

Y = Value of gross fish production;

$\overline{Y}$ = Geometric mean of the value of gross fish production;

X_i = i^{th} input;

$\overline{X}_i$ = Geometric mean of the ith input; and

β_i = Elasticity of production of the ith input./Regression coefficient of ith input.

An attempt was made to calculate 'F' values which would suggest whether the independent variables included in the study affected the fish production significantly or not. At the same time an attempt was also made to calculate production elasticities which determined the nature of returns to scale.

Finally marketing structure and its efficiency of the fish products in the study area was also studied by finding different marketing channels operating in the surveyed districts and marketing efficiency was also calculated with the help of the following formula:

$$ME = \frac{V}{I} - 1$$

where;

ME = Index of marketing efficiency

V = Value of goods sold (consumer's price)

I = Total marketing cost.

Limitations of the Study

In the State of Arunachal Pradesh the collection of both secondary and primary data is a very difficult task. Regarding, the secondary data, the researcher faced basically two problems. Firstly, the data related to fisheries is hardly available in published Statistical Abstract, etc. So, there was no other alternative but to collect from various relevant offices. However, the officials were reluctant to provide the necessary information required for any type of qualitative research. The problems are really acute in case of collection of primary data, since the transaction in the rural areas of the State are not yet fully monetized. Labour sharing, mutual assurance, barter system, community participation were common features in the study area. The magnitude of the problem was relatively high in the economy where production was meant mainly for home consumption and the level of monetization was low. The limitations which the researcher faced during the field survey were mainly due to the problems of measurement and problems of inadequate information. For example, in the measurement of agricultural output, including fish, the volume and not the standard weight is used. Till today, the common practice at the surveyed villages is the measurement of fishes by number. In order to examine the source of livelihood of the surveyed fish farmers, the measurement of agricultural output appeared to be necessary. However, in the measurement of agricultural output such as paddy, maize, millets, etc., the common unit of measurement is the number of basket; fruits, bamboo, etc., by numbers; and leafy vegetables, firewood, etc., by bundles. On the other hand measurement in the case of input in fish ponds like cow dung was by number of cows and banana leaf by the number of leaves. Therefore, the researcher needed to be familiar with the local units of measurement which required conversion.

Being an individual researcher and having resource constraint, it was difficult to conduct an extensive field survey and collect detailed information about the sampled households. In spite of these obstacles and constraints faced, the present study focuses on the ample opportunities for the development of fisheries in the State, based on the analysis of resource-use efficiency as well as the cost-benefit analysis. The socio-economic status of fish farmers, production and productivity of fish farming, livelihood options in fishery related activities and marketing structure in fishery are completely untouched areas of research in Arunachal Pradesh. Hence, this study tries to fill this gap in knowledge. In spite of limitations of data and obstacles faced by the researcher, it is hoped that the study will make a significant contribution in analyzing the opportunities and challenges of inland fisheries in Arunachal Pradesh, which is of crucial importance in income and employment generation for the people of the State.

Chapter Organisation

The Book is organized into seven chapters including the present introductory one which contains background of the study, objectives, research question framed, database and methodology, analytical framework, limitations and significance of the study.

The second chapter consists of review of the existing literature on fisheries related to productivity, livelihood strategy, resources-use efficiency, marketing structure, etc., and insights from empirical studies.

The third chapter contains a general discussion on the status of fisheries along with its trends, growth, etc., with special emphasis on the North Eastern Region of India and Arunachal Pradesh, i.e., the study area.

The fourth chapter includes a discussion on the background of the field study and a general profile of the surveyed districts. The important findings emerging from the analysis of the primary data like the socio-economic characteristics and livelihood linkages of the surveyed fish farmers as well as operational features of sampled ponds were incorporated here.

The fifth chapter contains an econometric analysis for determination of factors influencing the productivity of fisheries, as well as resource-use efficiency in the study area. It also includes the cost-benefit analysis and profitability estimates of fish farming in the study area. The issues relating to marketing structure and its efficiency are also taken up for detailed analysis.

In the sixth chapter an attempt is made to evaluate Government policies regarding fisheries as well as the constraints faced by the surveyed fish farmers.

The last chapter provides main findings and policy implications. The references followed by calculated data along with other related information including the questionnaire are provided in the appendix.

References

Choudhary *et al.* (2008): *Indigenous Knowledge and Policy Issues in Fisheries,* National Bureau of Fish Genetic Resources, ICAR, Lucknow.

Das, D. N. (2005): 'Utilisation of Fishery Resources in Arunachal Pradesh, India: An Overview of Socio-economic Dimension', in Tyagi, B. C. *et al.* (eds.), *Coldwater Fisheries Research and Development in North East Region of India,* National Research Centre on Coldwater Fisheries, Nainital, pp. 25-36.

Das, D. N., D. Sarma and P. C. Mahanta (2010): 'Scope for mountain fishery based eco-tourism in Arunachal Pradesh· Potential and recommendations', in Mahanta, P. C. and D. Sarma (eds.), *Coldwater Fisheries Management,* Directorate of Coldwater Fisheries Research, Nainital, pp. 285-296.

Government of Arunachal Pradesh (2011): *Statistical Abstract of Arunachal Pradesh,* Directorate of Economics and Statistics, Itanagar.

Government of Arunachal Pradesh (2012): *Statistical Abstract of Arunachal Pradesh,* Directorate of Economics and Statistics, Itanagar.

Government of India (2006): *Basic Statistics of North Eastern Region 2006,* North Eastern Council, Shillong.

Government of India (2006): *Report of the Working Group on Development and Management of Fisheries and Aquaculture for the XI Five Year Plan,* Planning Commission, New Delhi.

Government of India (2012): *Annual Report 2011-12,* Department of Animal Husbandry, Dairying & Fisheries, Ministry of Agriculture, New Delhi.

Government of India (2012): *Household Consumption of Various Goods and Services in India, 2004-05 NSS 66th Round (July 2009 - June 2010),* National Sample Survey Organisation, Ministry of Statistics and Programme Implementation, New Delhi.

Misra, S. R. (2012): *Sustainable Rural Livelihood Systems: The Case for India's Inland Fisheries Sector,* Concept Publishing Company (P) Ltd., New Delhi.

Mitra, A. (2005): 'Transformation of Arunachal's Economy: Opportunities and Challenges for a Less Developed State', *Indian Development Review,* Vol. 4, No. 2, pp. 433-440.

Sheperd, G.S. (1965). *Farm Products—Economic Analysis,* Iowa State University Press, Iowa, USA.

Chapter - 2

Productivity, Resource Use Efficiency, Livelihood Options and Marketing Structure in Fisheries

An Overview of Literatures

Introduction

The literature as well as information on various aspects of economics of inland fish cultivation were limited earlier, although much research work were done in the biological aspects of inland fisheries. One of the major reasons for the limited work in economics of inland fisheries may be due to lack of appropriate reliable data and standardized technologies necessary for comparability and aggregation of data over time and across regions. However, aquaculture which started since the eighties as primarily on Asian food production system has now spread to allcontinents. From an activity that was principally small scale, non-commercial and family-based, aquaculture now includes large-scale commercial and industrial production of high value species that are traded at regional, national and international levels. There is a wide consensus that aquaculture has the potential to meet the growing global demand for nutritious food, fish, and the contribution to the growth of the national economy, apart from supporting the sustainable livelihood of many communities (FAO, 2006). As a result, aquaculture practices are increasingly drawing attention of economists and social scientists during the last three decades. A number of studies related to economics of fish farming have been conducted by the economists and eminent social scientists at international level as well as national and State level in India. Some of these studies concentrated on evidences of structural and operational features under which fish production is practiced in tanks and ponds, resource-use efficiency of fisheries as well as the constraints faced by the fish farmers. In recent years, there is a growing interest in the studies on the livelihood issues of the people dependent on it, directly or indirectly. Hence, in this chapter, the survey of literature on economics of fisheries were conducted under the following sub-heads : (i) production and productivity of fisheries, (ii) resource use efficiency of fisheries, (iii) livelihood options of fisheries, and (iv) marketing structure of fisheries. The details were as follows:

Production and Productivity in Fishery

There were a number of studies done in the field of production and productivity of fisheries in national and international level.

Misra (2006) in his study explained that West Bengal had abundant natural resources and human skills for the development of fish farming. But in spite of enormous potential, much headway had not been achieved. The level of production had not been adequate leaving a large gap between actual and potential production level. According to him, the unsatisfactory performance could be responsible for all problems resulting in absence of rational management and judicious utilization of the resources. He finally concluded that, in order to protect the fisheries from increased in imports and at the same time to improve competitiveness in the global market, there was a need for reduction in the cost of production; increase in productivity and also to improve the quality of fish products.

Dey and Mahfuzuddin (2005) explained that there was no denying that the major factors driving the increase in productivity in Asia's aquaculture was the revolution in breeding, hatchery, and nursery technologies, together with a wide range of options in the production environment, feed, and species-mix. The result was the development of finfish aquaculture on millions of farm, the culture of low-to-mid-value species in a semi-intensive or extensive farming system, which used moderate to low levels of production inputs.

According to Sharma *et al.* (1998) modern aquaculture was a relatively new activity among the Nepalese farmers and was small contributor to the economy. Given the abundance of water resources and fish species, rising demand for fish, and its high profitability, aquaculture has the potential for future expansion if it is given appropriate attention from the government. In Nepal, productivity in aquaculture was much lower as compared to other countries in the region, which suggests that there was potential for increased fish production through technological progress and improvement in farm-level technical efficiency. Their study examined the production economics of Nepalese aquaculture, mainly focusing on technical efficiency of carp pond culture. The production data and farm specific information were collected from a sample of carp producers which were analysed using a stochastic production frontier, including a model for the technical inefficiency effects. They also highlighted farming system, profitability and problems associated with carp production. The output and input variables were measured in per hectare terms. The parameters for the production frontier and those for the technical inefficiency model were estimated simultaneously using a maximum likelihood estimation technique. They concluded that there were significant production inefficiencies among the sampled carp producers in Nepal. The tests conducted by them indicated that the farm-specific variables were highly significant in explaining technical inefficiencies for fish farmers, especially production intensity and the adoption of management practices.

The main objective of a study undertaken by Sharma (1999) was to examine the technical efficiency and its determinants in carp pond culture in Pakistan. A stochastic production frontier involving the model for technical inefficiency effects was applied separately to the samples of semi-intensive, intensive and extensive carp producers. The aquaculture was a relatively new, but rapidly expanding activity in the country. Despite its small contribution to the national economy, aquaculture has become an increasingly important sector in terms of its potential for increasing domestic supply of fish protein in the country. The study examined the technical efficiencies of semi intensive, intensive and extensive carp producers in Pakistan. The production data and relevant farm-specific variables collected from the samples of semi-intensive, intensive and extensive farms were analysed separately using a Cobb-Douglas stochastic production frontier, including a model for technical inefficiency effects. The results showed the presence of significant technical inefficiencies among the sampled carp farms, which could be explained in terms of various farm specific variables, such as adoption of management practices, total pond area and farm location. The adoption of recommended fish, water and feed management practices had a positive impact on technical efficiency. The pond area had a negative influence on the performance of the farms both under semi-intensive, intensive and extensive systems.

In a paper Dey *et al.* (2005) reviewed the status of freshwater aquaculture and analyzed the factors that explained fish production and fish demand in selected Asian countries of India, Bangladesh and Thailand, to identify appropriate technologies suitable for poor fish farmers in the region. Over the last two decades, there has been a significant improvement in aquaculture technologies that are being used in these countries. The recent technological innovation also allowed aquaculture in paddy fields, running waters, and sewage-fed water. The results of the production function analysis revealed that even the semi-intensive methods were below optimum resource allocation in the poly-culture of carps. The farmers in Bangladesh and India experienced decreasing marginal productivity of farm-based feed where these are used in excessive quantity. On the other hand, the farmers in Thailand had increasing marginal productivity for both energy and protein even at higher levels of production due to the application of balanced feeds.

Schwindt *et al.* (2000) in their study applied cost-benefit analysis to the Canadian Pacific commercial salmon fishery. They demonstrated that Government policies to preserve the fishery have resulted in higher net social costs than would have resulted from a 'does nothing' policy, notwithstanding the rent dissipation associated with unconstrained resource exploitation. The value of landings and the private costs of the harvest over a cycle were also calculated by them.

Nepal has a dense net of rivers and streams, as well as numerous lakes of cold water character. Shrestha (2002) analysed that fish stocks in these waters were undergoing changes as a result of overfishing, poor land management resulted in siltation, damming, pollution and some other adverse impacts. The potential of cold water fisheries was not fully utilized and it was believed that with proper management, introducing innovative methods, especially in the direction of a better protection of fish stocks, their enhancement through controlled and protected spawning, habitat improvements and some other management measures, the cold water fishery resources can be brought to a level which will allow their sustainable harvesting without further harming the fish stocks.

Oo, W. (2002) analysed that in the fiscal year 2000-2001 cold water capture fisheries production was 7,711 tonnes, aquaculture 2,848 tonnes, as compared to the total inland capture fisheries production of 2,35,373 tonnes, aquaculture 1,09,188 tonnes, plus 6,603 tonnes of prawn production from aquaculture in Myanmar. The cold water fishery resources are poorly known as there were virtually no surveys and research done in recent years. Cold water fish are an important source of protein for the hilly people, and there is an urgent need for cold water fisheries development with the assistance of international organizations. Fish consumption in Myanmar is 21 kg per head per year. Poor management of capture fisheries is threatening the fish supply in the near future. There was need for more effective management of fisheries. But the management must be fitted to the prevailing fisheries status of the country. The approach to fisheries management must also change from the conventional system to a more appropriate management system. The Government has to take responsibility to ensure that effective measures are implemented.

Raimiyar (1998) in his study suggested a substantial gap between knowledge and adoption of management and technological practices by fishpond operators in Nepal. His research also indicated that the practices examined were not independent of one another. The years of schooling and distance from fish market were dominant variables. The household size was an important variable in the adoption of input-related and record-keeping-related practices. Total cultivable land area, explained variation in input-related, physical characteristics and integration with other farming enterprises; while fishpond water surface area was an important consideration in the adoption of fish seed-related, input-related, physical characteristics and other management-related practices. The private ownership of fishponds was associated with the adoption of fish seed and input-related practices. Furthermore, the use of private sources of information contributed to the increased adoption of other management-related practices.

Resource Use Efficiency in Fishery

There are various methodologies utilized to evaluate the efficiency of aquaculture production system. Based on Farrell's innovative article (1957), several approaches to efficiency and productivity assessment were developed that can be classified into two broad categories, i.e., (i) parameters, and (ii) non-parameters frontier models. The first one depending on the specification of an *ad hoc* functional form imposes certain *a priori* restrictions on the production on the cost function statistically. Alternatively, the latter constructs a linear piecewise function from empirical observation of inputs and outputs, thereby avoiding the need to assume functional relationship between inputs and outputs or to make distributional assumption regarding residuals in a regression analysis. Some of the important studies reviewed were as follows:

In a study by Ogundari and Ojo (2009), they examined income generation potential and resource-use efficiency of 120 aquaculture farms in Oyo state of Nigeria. The data collected were analysed using gross margin and stochastic frontier production model. The study examined the potential inherent in aquaculture production in alleviating households' income poverty in the country. Gross-margin to access profitability of the farms as well as stochastic frontier production model to measure resources-use efficiency of the farms was employed for the analysis. Based on their study they concluded the following: first, aquaculture production is a profitable investment considering the size, gross-margin, obtained from the study. Secondly, the farms were fairly efficient in the use of their resources considering the size of technical efficiency obtained. Finally, they found that promotion of aquaculture development had the potential in alleviating household income poverty.

The paper by Inoni, O.E. (2007) examined the production function approach to the efficiency of resource utilisation in pond fish production in Delta State of Nigeria. Regression results indicated that pond size, feeds, fingerlings, and labour were significant determinants of output in pond fish production. The index of resource-use efficiency revealed that fish farmers were not only inefficient in the allocation of productive resources, but grossly over-utilized feeds, fingerlings, fixed costs, and labour.

Anene *et al.* (2010) in their study determined the cost-returns and the efficiency of resources used in artisanal fishing by fishers in Oguta Local Government Area of Imo State Nigeria. The research identified that artisanal fishing was profitable and all the factors employed were inefficiently utilized. The study suggested that higher profit and yields could be attained by efficient allocation of the employed resources which was vital to the sustainability of fishing in Nigeria.

Zen *et al.* (2002) in a study examined the production structure of the multi-species, multi-gear fishery in West Sumatra, Indonesia. Majority of the fishermen in the area were living below the poverty level. This phenomenon was often attributed to low productivity and inefficient use of fishing inputs. Two important fishing gears, *driftnet* and *Payang seine* (lampara) were chosen for the study. They analysed that expansion in fish production for driftnet fishery was still possible by adopting the technology of the highly experienced or well-trained fishermen and through optimal resource allocation, although lampara fishery had been operating at the optimal level. The policies to increase fish catch should, therefore, be focused on driftnet fishing, while effort reduction measures on the other hand should be imposed on lampara fishery.

According to Ali (1990) the rice-fish farming system in Malaysia required no biological and little economic input, and native fish were found to be both biologically and economically suitable. The system utilized different specific habitats; the fish were tolerant to extreme physico-chemical changes, and command good market prices. Aquatic productivity of the prevailing ecosystem was low despite repeated seasonal fertilization. Productivity was probably low due to shading and competition with aquatic weeds and rice plants. Zooplankton was not readily available to the fish larvae and fingerlings because aquatic weeds provided easy refuge. This lack of food resulted in fish below marketable size. The short growing season resulting from double cropping, coupled with widespread use of herbicides and pesticides, also affected fish production. Several improvements in management for this type of farming system were recommended.

In a study Emokaro and Ekunwe (2009) employed the use of the stochastic frontier production function in the empirical analysis of efficiency of resource-use and elasticity of production among catfish farmers in Kaduna, Nigeria. They found that catfish farmers in the study area were not efficient in their use of production inputs. It was also found that catfish farmers in Kaduna were not efficient in their use of production resources. While labour and fingerlings were underutilized, pond size was overutilized and catfish feed grossly overutilized. The result was further confirmed by the positive decreasing return to scale as evidenced by the return to scale estimated, indicated that catfish production in the study area was still in stage two of the production process. They suggested the existence of intervention points by relevant stakeholders in the current production technology of catfish farmers in the study area. Such effort would aid in the transfer of more economically efficient production technologies that would enhance the current level of efficiency of catfish farmers in the study area. Such interventions include special funding targeted towards the development of cheaper alternative sources of production, inputs like catfish feed, and construction of economic-size ponds.

Bush and Kosy (2007) in an article provided a detailed empirical analysis of investment patterns in small-scale rural aquaculture and its relation to pond location based on a systematic fish pond survey in Lao PDR. Nominal investment categories of fish ponds were created based on stocking-rate, feed and water and then spatially cross-referenced with a range of environmental factors, including distance to roads, land-use, and distance to water resources. They concluded that policy makers and extension officers can make use of simple diagnostic models of fish pond use and investment to develop more contingent support to farmers that takes into consideration a wider portfolio of living aquatic resources in rural communities. The results of the study indicated that fish ponds were a complex and diverse aquatic resource with a range of stocking strategies involving both exotic and native species.

Livelihood Options in Fishery

The subject of livelihood enhancement and diversification among different fishing communities has been debated since the early

1980's, especially when doubt started cropping up about the livelihood of the poor. In search of an alternative, promotion for livelihood strategy has become popular policy to uplift the socio-economic status of fisheries. In the early 1990's, people centred subsistence oriented sustainable livelihood approach (SLA) emerged as a meaningful policy option to address the context of livelihood enhancement and diversification of fishing communities. Some of the studies regarding livelihood diversification as well as other options are given below:

Phillips *et al.* (2002) in an article analysed some environmental and socio-economic aspects to be considered in the development of aquaculture and cold water fisheries in the Hindu Kush — Himalayan region. Indigenous fish species living within the Hindu Kush—Himalayan region represent an important aquatic resource for the sub-Himalayan region. Unfortunately, the resource was generally unrecognized and undervalued and has so far been given limited consideration in rural development. Experiences available within highland areas in Asia suggested that there was potential for aquaculture and fisheries development to contribute to rural development and poverty alleviation.

Allison (2007) reviewed the importance of fisheries to livelihoods in 'wetlands in dry lands' with a focus on case-studies in Africa. The study examined the threats posed by climate change to the traditional 'tri-economy' of fishing, farming and livestock herding. Although both livelihood strategies and local institutions were highly adapted to cope with, and benefit from, climate-induced variability, weaknesses in the wider governance and macro-economic environment mean that the overall adaptive capacity of these regions was low and the farmer-herder-fishers were vulnerable to projected climate change. In order to maintain the important nutritional, economic, cultural and social benefits of fisheries in the face of climate change, planned adaptation at scales from the local to the regional was required. The concept of resilience in linked social-ecological systems to examine how such responses could be developed and promoted was analysed in the study.

Nam and Roitana (2005) in a report explained that the inland capture fisheries of Cambodia was rich and valuable resources providing a vital contribution to the livelihood for rural areas, generating family income, employing up to 2 million people and contributing to national economy.

Viner *et al.* (2006) explained although there was potential for successful co-management in Cambodian small-scale fisheries, it was currently limited by some important constraints. These include the lack of clearly defined enabling legislation, of property rights, of resource boundaries and of access control. Additionally, management objectives were, in some cases, inappropriate and there was little agreement among co-management partners, on whether the objective was improving sustainability in the fishery or maintaining rural livelihoods. The study concluded that unless alternative livelihood options become available and more attractive than fishing to resource users, fishing pressure was likely to remain high, with resultant low catch per unit effort and low individual catches.

A survey was conducted by Zaman *et al.* (2006) in Mohanpur Upazila, Rajshahi, Bangladesh to determine the pond fishery resources and the livelihood status of fish farmers. Fish farmers were found to face various problems such as social, economic and technical problems, which were identified during the study. They concluded that fish farmers should be given facilities on training programme, and input availabilities. Fish farmers should also be provided with credit facilities, motivated to utilize all types of water bodies for fish culture as well as integrated culture should be adopted. The fish farmers should also be given amenities for education so that they can be well aware of their problems and prime rights. All the water resources should be utilized for fish culture to get maximum production by using suitable technology. More hatcheries should be established, so that fish farmers can get quality seeds easily.

Gurung *et al.* (2005) in a paper deals with the participatory fisheries management programme, aimed at and successful in livelihood improvement of fisherman community known as *'Pode'* or *'Jalari'* living near Phewa Lake, Pokhara, Nepal. The community, traditionally depend on fishing activities for their livelihood, led a nomadic life along the rivers and lakes, carrying cast nets to feed their families. It was anticipated that fish farmers can contribute to the sustainable management of Phewa Lake, if they are allowed to participate fully and share their skills and traditional knowledge. Since, the participatory management of natural resources in Phewa Lake has been proved to be an important avenue for sustainable livelihood enhancement of poor, it was also anticipated that several other water bodies could be wisely managed to bring deprived fisher communities into the mainstream of society.

Ahmed (2009) applied the Sustainable Livelihoods Approach (SLA) to understand the role of fish farming in Mymensingh area of north-central Bangladesh. The study used the SLA framework as an analytical tool to identify ways to advance the livelihoods of fish farmers. He finally concluded that fish farmers can achieve sustainable livelihoods through access to a range of livelihood assets.

Misra, S. (2012) explained that most of the impoundment ponds and tanks do not retain water throughout the year in the State of West Bengal. In the post-winter, depth of the water becomes less than the minimum required for fish farming. Farmers are forced to harvest juvenile uneconomic varieties belonging to different size-groups. As a result, they could not fetch a commercially viable market price. He suggested that if fish farming was being developed in order to alleviate poverty, it could be realised that the poor fish farmers had only small and relatively unproductive ponds. If the Government want to reduce the poverty then they could take the lead in that aspects and seriously review the objectives of on-going strategies and further design planned mechanism for fishery sector.

Marketing Structure in Fishery

Marketing plays a very crucial role in economic development as it increases production, avoids unnecessary fluctuation in output and prices and reduced cost of production. Unlike many agricultural and industrial products, fresh fish is not treated as a well-defined commodity. Fish is a highly perishable product with unpredictable supply. In order to make the fish available to consumers at reasonable prices, at right time and place it requires an effective marketing system. Therefore, fish marketing is a vital aspect for sellers, consumers and other facilitating agencies including the Government.

Kumar *et al.* (2010) in a paper described the highly efficient fish marketing system prevalent in the Kolleru Lake area (KLA) and compared it to the marketing of Indian Major Carps (IMC) in other major aquaculture states like West Bengal and Orissa and marine states like Maharashtra and Tamil Nadu. The marketing channels, market intermediaries, price spread and marketing efficiency in the study area were analysed. A comparison of the marketing channels at several fish markets has revealed that the price spread for IMC from Kolleru was highest at the Mumbai market and lowest at the Coimbatore market.

Roy (2008) analysed the existing marketing status of fish fingerlings with special reference to environmental concerns and awareness of the fishermen. He identified the constraints and suggested measures for the development of marketing of fishery on the basis of primary data collected from Dakshin Dinajpur district of West Bengal. His study revealed that the degree of consciousness among respondents about the environment and its impact on fish production and marketing was limited. Infrastructural facilities and information dissemination about marketing are the two very important issues which needed immediate attentions.

Kumar *et al.* (2008) conducted a study in all the major coastal States and some selected inland States to understand the domestic marketing of fishes in India. They found that though domestic fish marketing holds a huge potential, it was still highly unorganized and unregulated in India. It was neglected for various reasons and serious efforts were not made for marketing of fishes as compared to its production. The improvement in fish marketing system and distribution was not only reduced the demand-supply gap of fishes across the country, but it also contributed to food and nutritional security of a vast majority of lower income group population.

Alam *et al.* (2010) conducted a study at fish marketing system in Swarighat, Dhaka, Bangladesh, which analysed the existing marketing system, economic features of marketing activities and inefficiencies. The study also attempted to identify infrastructure facilities, present market structure, nature of costs, profit margins and the factor that influence the marketing system. In the study area, almost all fish traded internally move through the private sector where a large number of people are dealing with fish distribution and marketing system. The market chain from producers to retailers goes onward through a number of intermediaries like traders, broker, *aratdar*, wholesalers, *mahajans*, and *dadondars*. They concluded that, for increasing the productivity of fish farmers and making certain about their livelihood security, an efficient fish marketing system was a vital requisite.

Olubunmi and Bankole (2012) conducted a study to assess the market structure, the socio-economic characteristics of the fish marketers and determinants of revenue generated from fish marketing in Ibarapa area, Oyo State, Nigeria using purposive sampling, which cut across age, and gender of fish sellers in each location. They found that fish marketing was a profitable business in the study area especially frozen fish which most of the people in the area preferred. Their study revealed that the major determinant of revenue generated from fish marketed was average price of fish, transportation cost and duration of sales per day. According to them storage problem was the major problem facing by the fish marketers in Ibarapa. A large proportion of losses associated with this sector might reduce if fish sellers had cooperative associations to take advantage of economies of scale of production like collective buying and selling, investing in storage facilities which can maintain quality of product and hence give higher return to sellers. Smoked fish processing should be improved by providing kilns at affordable prices to processors who should be trained on good manufacturing practices. There was need for improvement in major towns in the study area in terms of the provision of infrastructures such as electricity and storage facilities.

Other Important Studies

Other than production, livelihood, resource-use efficiency and marketing there were other important studies; some of them are discussed in the following sub-section:

Ayyappan and Krishna (2004) made an attempt to review the production potentials and export possibilities of Indian fish production. They suggested different measures to meet the domestic requirement with a view to emphasizing on earning reasonable amount of foreign exchange by way of extensive export measures.

Kumar and Dey (2004) analysed the long-term changes that took place in fish consumption in India. An attempt was also made to study the demand modelling on multistage budgeting framework and examined the demand elasticity for fish. The responsiveness of demand for fish to change in price and income varies for fish-income classes, regions and urbanization. Own price-elasticity of demand for fish was higher and has not shown any sign of declining during the last fifteen years.

Misra, S. (1987), in his book revealed that poaching acted as a major constraint leading to poor performance of fish production particularly in West Bengal's tanks and ponds. On the basis of data collected from tank and pond owners in three districts of West Bengal, he arrived at the conclusion that poaching or deliberate poisoning due to rivalry, enmity or jealousy are widespread. Among other problems, lack of proper transport facility, suitable marketing management, non-availability of opportunity for soil and water testing, etc., were considered by the poor fishermen as the major inhibiting factors. In consideration to non-adoption of new techniques, he observed that lack of information regarding various improved practices is one of the important factors. The financial difficulties due to bureaucratic delay, etc., made the practice of composite fish-farming technologies much more difficult. Other problems were erratic and inadequate supply of quality fish seeds or fingerlings in time and at reasonable rate, multiple ownership and adulteration of inputs. The measures suggested by him are the utilization of canal irrigation or rainfed farming on watershed basis, desalting of about to dry-up ponds, long term lease arrangement, Government legislation to evict multiple ownership, development of appropriate technologies, organized marketing channels, mixed farming etc.

Dey's (2000) analysis was based on a matrix of price and income elasticities of demand for fish by type, as fish was a heterogeneous product and consumption patterns may differ by type of products. The study estimated fish demand elasticities by fish type for Bangladesh. Income elasticities of all fish types consistently fell with the increase in per capita expenditure level of households, but none of the fish types become an inferior good at the highest income quartile.

Li and Huang (2005) in their paper reviewed recent developments in China's fishery and aquaculture sectors, as well as the policies affecting rural households in general, and fisheries households in particular. It explored how China's policies may change as a result of the nation joining the World Trade Organization in December 2001 and the likely impacts of these changes on China's fishery and aquaculture sector. They found that the domestic fish markets are gradually integrating, suggesting that fish price shifts in one area will affect prices in most parts of the country. They found that, compared with the prices of other agricultural commodities; the domestic prices of most aquatic products are well below world prices. They suggested that exports of aquatic products would be able to expand now that the nation has joined the WTO and that fisherman would gain from this move. As the largest producer of fishery products and aquaculture in the world, China's industry was one of the few subsectors that have been maintaining rapid growth, in line with overall economic development. It has become the largest exporter within China's agriculture sector.

Yaqoob (2002) explained that the stocks of indigenous fish were threatened by overfishing and deterioration of the environment in Pakistan. Exotic brown trout has established self-reproducing stocks in a number of rivers, and the rainbow trout was cultured. Indigenous fish protection and domestication are major priorities. Raising awareness among the local population of the need to protect fishery resources and social uplift of fisherman are two major areas for future action. According to him, other needs are the establishment of a database management system, and encouraging regional cooperation and networking to resolved issues of common interest.

Floodplain fisheries make an important contribution to the total freshwater catches of Africa. Rules and institutions controlling access to these fisheries have received little attention in the literature. The paper by Thomas (1996) explored property regimes operating in the *Hadejia-Jama'are* floodplain fishery, Nigeria, with a focus on a case-study village. Private, communal property and open-access tenure regimes existed. The physical characteristics of the resources under each of these categories are differentiated. The economic cost of making resources more exclusive appeared to be a key factor affecting tenure. According to the study, the social benefits of communal access are also extremely important. In a risky environment that was characterized by spatial and temporal variation in the distribution of resources, maintaining rights of access to a wide geographical portfolio of resources is an important consideration. This was especially true considering recent environmental changes in the floodplain caused by dams and drought.

The study by Dey *et al.* (2005) discussed fish consumption and preference patterns for fish species by income groups, and by urban and rural divide in Bangladesh, China, India, Indonesia, the Philippines, Thailand, and Vietnam. The fish consumption varied widely with economic position of the households, in terms of both per capita consumption and type of fish species. They found the, firstly, the per capita fish consumption increased with increase in income. Secondly, the share of fish protein in total animal protein expenditure was higher for lower income groups, demonstrating their dependence on fish as a source of animal protein. Thirdly, poor people consumed mostly low-price fish and rich people spent a significant portion of their fish budget on expensive fish. Finally, the per capita fish consumption was substantially higher in rural areas than in urban areas.

Studies in North Eastern Region of India and Arunachal Pradesh

The North Eastern Region of India has a large potential for development of inland water fisheries. Many studies were conducted by scientists of the region to explain the potential and status of aquaculture in the region. Some of the important findings were given below:

Das (2002) did an excellent work regarding the rice fish production systems. He found that fish were harvested from rice fields as an additional crop since ancient times. Biologically, rice fields can be considered as agriculturally managed marshes, which remain dry for varying periods of time during the year. Physically, the aquatic phase has varying water depth according to the land topography and local rainfall patterns and water tables. In its flooded state, the rice field was a rich and productive biological system which can produce a crop of aquatic organisms, both plant and animal, for human consumption in addition to the rice. The farmers of the North Eastern part of India in all the seven States cultivate rice as their staple food. The ecology of their rice fields in the region is quite diverse, but can be divided primarily into upland, lowland and deep water rice ecosystems. On the basis of water sources there are two types of fields, viz., irrigated and rain fed rice fields. In this region of the country, a fish crop was traditionally raised only from the paddies of rain fed lowlands (both shallow and deep water). In many areas, irrigation fed rice fields have also been adapted locally by the farmers to include fish farming. Traditional rice-fish production systems have an important socio-economic part in the life of the farmers and fishermen in the region.

Barik and Katiha (2003) opined that the floodplain wetlands are the prime fisheries resources of Assam. Although, it is a sensitive ecosystem, it contributed significantly to the stability and sustenance, if managed efficiently. The vastness and responsiveness to the manipulations generate enormous opportunities to harness their economic benefits, which could be explained from the existing gap between the potential and realised productivity. The two options realised the potential, viz., technological and institutional are complementary to each other. But, the institutional set-up holds the key in the attainment of other management objectives besides the potential realisation. The role of Government was limited only to ownership and lease, despite the complex system of diverse institutions and organisations. More active participation of State machinery in setting and implementation of policies, regulations and providing incentives for productivity and efficiency were required. The appropriate functioning, cordination of other institutions like fishing groups, lessees, bankers, commission agents, etc., are vital in management of *beels*. This can be achieved through development of institutional mechanism for the information sharing and collective action. Above all, the orientation towards shared interest will go a long way in realising the management objectives of this resource. These will in turn, generate larger economic and social benefits to the State in general, and people in particular.

Das (2005) in another study emphasised that there was expanding need for socio-economic information on the part of the policy-makers and the planners for the development of fishery. According to him the issue has received little importance in India, more particular in the North Eastern India including Arunachal Pradesh. The study highlighted the potential that lies with the scope of judicious utilization of fishery resources of a State which is rich in biodiversity.

According to Saikia and Das (2008) rice-based fish farming, though, inevitable as a mean of double crop production from the unit land, was often found as cost-effective practice for marginal and poor farmers. The novel technique adopted by *Apatani* farmers in Lower Subansiri district of Arunachal Pradesh, India reduces the knowledge gap to achieve optimum benefit from such farming practiced. The farmers enjoyed a fish productivity of 500 kg per hectare per year without providing any supplementary feed to the fish stocked in their rice-fields. The economic return of the farmers was estimated up to 65.8 per cent per annum from their rice-fish integrated fields. The system of rice-based fish farming by *Apatani* farmers has, therefore, bears immense potential to be recognized as low cost and sustainable farming practice and could be a significant breakthrough for poor and marginal farmers of the rest of the world.

Moda (2005) explained that a fishery is not only having social relevance, but it was also an economic activity in the State. With the ever growing population, besides unemployment scenario, there was a need to strengthen the fishery in cold water zone.

In a study Debnath *et al.* (2009) explained the nature of resources available and how they were combined and utilized in aquaculture largely determine its economic viability and social profitability. Using Resource Cost Ratio (RCR), they analysed resource-use efficiency and social profitability of an integrated aqua farm located in Tripura.

According to Goswami *et al.* (2002) fish marketing is a flourishing trade in the economy of Assam as it was one of the most preferred food items of the State's population. There is a wide gap between the present supply and requirement of fish, which was partially met by the supply from other fish producing States. The distribution process of fresh fish, dried fish and fish seed was analysed. Women were also found to be involved in the retail trade in the markets and door to door sales in some selected parts of Kamrup District. According to them a well organised marketing network was essential for distribution of fish in the State at reasonable price. The study highlighted the prevailing marketing system, market channels, market availability and market-related constraints in the growth of fish marketing in the State.

In an attempt Nath, D. (1996) outlined the growth and development of pisciculture and its significance in the economic life of *Apatani* people of Arunachal Pradesh. He explained the steps required to improve the production of fisheries and to create permanent source of income for the people in a scientific way. His study finally suggested for optimising the resource allocation, mobilisation and implementation of various development programmes regarding fisheries for better result.

Mandal, S. *et al.* (2007) analysed the economic and financial viabilities of development of ornamental fisheries in the North Eastern region. They concluded that the agribusiness opportunities can be realized at every stage, namely, production, marketing and conservation of ornamental fishes. The ornamental fish production in the North East India has been observed to be financially as well as economically viable and investment-friendly. With the initiatives by the government such as providing incentives to establish ornamental fish production unit, considerable private investment can be attracted to this industry, which would generate additional employment opportunities in the area. According to them concerted efforts of the government as well as key institutions can increase the ornamental fish production substantially in the region, which in turn, can gain a larger share in the world market. Public-private partnership can be encouraged through establishment of ornamental fish production units in different parts of the North East India to make the ornamental fishery sector more vibrant and remunerative.

From the above survey of literature, it was found that economics of fisheries did not receive much attention from the researchers of the North Eastern Region of India. So, very few studies were conducted in the region regarding, the production, resource use efficiency and marketing structure of inland fisheries in the region which has a large potential for upliftment of economic condition of the poor people. Hence, the present study is an attempt to fill this gap in knowledge.

References

Ahmed, N. *et al.* (2009) : "The Sustainable Livelihoods Approach to the Development of Freshwater Prawn Marketing Systems in Southwest Bangladesh", *Aquaculture Economics and Management*, Vol. 13, No. 3, pp. 246-269.

Alam, J. Md. *et al.* (2010): "A Study on Fish Marketing System in Swarighat, Dhaka, Bangladesh", *Nature and Science*, Vol. 8, No. 12, pp. 96-103.

Ali, A. B. (1990): "Rice/Fish Farming in Malaysia: A Resource Optimization", *Ambio*, Vol. 19, No. 8, pp. 404-408.

Allison, E. H. *et al.* (2007): "Enhancing the Resilience of Inland Fisheries and Aquaculture Systems to Climate Change", *SAT e Journal*, Vol. 4, Is. 1.

Anene, A. *et al.* (2010): "Resources Use and Efficiency of Artisanal Fishing in Oguta, Imo State, Nigeria", *Journal of Development and Agricultural Economics*, Vol. 2, No. 3, pp. 094-099.

Ayyappan, S. and M. Krishna (2004), "Fisheries Sector in India: Dimensions of Development", *Indian Journal of Agricultural Economics*, Volume 59, No. 3, pp. 392-411.

Barik, N. K. and P. K. Katiha (2003): "Management of Fisheries of Floodplain Wetlands: Institutional Issues and Options for Assam", in Kumar, A. *et al.* (eds.), *A Profile of People, Technologies and Policies in Fisheries Sector in India*, Workshop Proceedings Series 10, National Centre for Agricultural Economics and Policy Research, New Delhi, pp. 141-157.

Bush, S. R. and S. Kosy (2007): "Geographical Distribution of Investment in Small-Scale Rural Fish Ponds", *Aquaculture Economics and Management*, Vol. 11, No. 3, pp. 285-311.

Das, D. N. (2002): "Fish Farming in Rice Environments of North Eastern India", *Aquaculture Asia*, Vol. VII No. 2, pp. 43-47.

Das, D. N. (2005): "Utilisation of Fishery Resources in Arunachal Pradesh, India: An Overview of Socio-economic Dimension", in Tyagi, B. C. *et al.* (eds.), *Coldwater Fisheries Research and Development in North East Region of India*, National Research Centre on Coldwater Fisheries, Nainital, pp. 25-36.

Debnath, B. et al. (2009): "Resource Use Efficiency and Social Profitability of an Integrated Aqua-Farm, Tripura, India", *Aquaculture Economics and Management*, Vol. 13, No. 4, pp. 344-354.

Dey, M. M. (2000): "Analysis of demand for fish in Bangladesh", *Aquaculture Economics and Management*, Vol. 4, No. 1, pp. 63-81.

Dey, M. M. and A. Mahfuzuddin (2005): "Aquaculture-Food and Livelihoods for the Poor in Asia: A Brief Overview of the Issues", *Aquaculture Economics and Management*, Vol. 9, No. 1, pp.1-10.

Dey, M. M. *et al.* (2005): "Status and Economics of Freshwater Aquaculture in Selected Countries of Asia", *Aquaculture Economics and Management*, Vol. 9, No. 1, pp. 11-37.

Emokaro, C. O. and P. A. Ekunwe (2009): "Efficiency of resource-use and elasticity of production among catfish farmers in Kaduna, Nigeria", *African Journal of Biotechnology*, Vol. 8, No. 25, pp. 7249-7252.

FAO (2006): *The State of World Fisheries and Aquaculture*, FAO, UN, Rome.

Farrell, M.J.(1957): The Measurement of Productive Efficiency, Journal of Royal Statistical Society. Series A (General), Vol. 120, No. pp. 253-290.

Goswami, M. *et al.* (2002): "Market Flow, Price Structure and Fish Marketing System in Assam- A Case Study", in *Proceedings of National Conference on Fisheries Economics, Extension and Management*, CIFE, Mumbai.

Gurung, T. B. et al. (2005): "Participatory Fisheries Management for Livelihood Improvement of Fishers in Phewa Lake, Pokhara, Nepal", *Himalayan Journal of Sciences*, Vol. 3, Is. 5, pp. 47-52.

Inoni, O.E. (2007): "Allocative Efficiency in Pond Fish Production in Delta State, Nigeria: A Production Function Approach", *Agricultura Tropica ET Subtropica*, Vol. 40, No. 4, pp. 127-134.

Kumar, B. G. et al. (2008): "Domestic Fish Marketing in India-Changing Structure, Conduct, Performance and Policies", *Agricultural Economics Research Review*, Vol. 21(Conference Number), pp. 345-354.

Kumar, B. G. *et al.* (2010): "Marketing System and Efficiency of Indian Major Carps in India", *Agricultural Economics Research Review*, Vol. 23, pp. 105-113.

Kumar, P. and M. M. Dey (2004): "A Study of Modelling of Household Demand for Fisheries in India", *Indian Journal of Agricultural Economics*, Vol. 59, No.3, pp. 465-475.

Li, L. and J. Huang (2005): "China's Accession to the WTO and Its Implications for the Fishery and Aquaculture Sector", *Aquaculture Economics and Management*, Vol. 9, No. 1, pp. 195-215.

Mandal, S. *et al.* (2007): "Agribusiness Opportunities of Ornamental Fisheries in North-Eastern Region of India", *Agricultural Economics Research Review*, Vol. 20 (Conference Issue), pp. 471-488.

Misra, S. R. (1987): *Fisheries in India*, Ashis Publishing House, New Delhi.

Misra, S. R. (2006): *Inland Fisheries in India: Issues and Concerns*, Concept Publishing Company, New Delhi.

Misra, S. R. (2012): *Sustainable Rural Livelihood Systems: The Case for India's Inland Fisheries Sector*, Concept Publishing Company (P) Ltd., New Delhi.

Moda, T. (2005): "Status Paper on Fisheries of Arunachal Pradesh", in Tyagi, B. C. *et al.* (eds.), *Coldwater Fisheries Research and Development in North East Region of India*, National Research Centre on Coldwater Fisheries, Nainital, pp.139-144.

Nam, S. and B. Roitana (2005): "A Review of Inland Fisheries Management in Cambodia", *Asian Productivity Organization (APO) and the International Seminar on Inland Fisheries Management*, 21-26 September 2005, New Delhi, India.

Nath, D. (1996): "Significance of Fisheries in the Life of Apatani Tribe", *Arunachal University Research Journal*, Vol. 1, pp. 86-97.

Ogundari, K. and S.O. Ojo (2009): "An Examination of Income Generation Potential of Aquaculture Farms in Alleviating Household Poverty: Estimation and Policy Implications from", *Turkish Journal of Fisheries and Aquatic Sciences*, Vol. 9, pp. 39-45.

Olubunmi, A. and A. F. Bankole (2012): "Determinants of Income from Fish Marketing in Ibarapa Area of Oyo State, Nigeria", *Science Journal of Agricultural Research and Management*, Vol. 2012, Article ID sjarm-135, p. 6.

Oo, W. (2002): "Inland Fisheries of the Union of Myanmar", in Petr, T. and Swar, D.B. (eds.) *Cold Water Fisheries in the Trans-Himalayan Countries*, FAO Fisheries Technical Paper, No. 431, FAO, Rome, pp. 70-76.

Phillips, M. J. *et al.* (2002): "Environment, Livelihoods and Indigenous Cold Water Fishes" in Petr, T. and Swar, D.B. (eds.) *Cold Water Fisheries in the Trans-Himalayan Countries*, FAO Fisheries Technical Paper, No. 431, FAO, Rome, pp. 39-46.

Raimiyar, G. P. (1998): "Adoption of Management and Technological Practices by Fishpond Operators in Nepal", *Aquaculture Economics and Management*, Vol. 2, No. 3, pp. 89-99.

Roy, T. N. (2008): "Analysis of Marketing of Fish Fingerlings and Environmental Awareness Level of Fishermen in Dakshin Dinajpur District of West Bengal", *Agricultural Economics Research Review*, Vol. 21 (Conference Number), pp. 425-432.

Saikia, S. K. and D. N. Das (2008): "Rice-Fish Culture and its Potential in Rural Development: A Lesson from Apatani Farmers, Arunachal Pradesh, India", *Journal of Agriculture and Rural Development*, Vol. 6, No. (1 & 2), pp. 125-131.

Schwindt, R. *et al.* (2000): "Net Loss: A Cost-Benefit Analysis of the Canadian Pacific Salmon Fishery", *Journal of Policy Analysis and Management*, Vol. 19, No. 1, pp. 23-45.

Sharma, K. R. (1999): "Technical Efficiency of Carp Production in Pakistan", *Aquaculture Economics and Management*, Vol. 3, No. 2, pp. 131-141.

Sharma, K. R. *et al.* (1998): "Technical Efficiency of Carp Production in

Nepal: An Application of Stochastic Frontier Production Function Approach", *Aquaculture Economics and Management*, Vol. 2, No. 3, pp. 129-140.

Shrestha, T.K. (2002): "Cold Water Fisheries Development in Nepal", in Petr, T. and Swar, D.B. (eds.) *Cold Water Fisheries in the Trans-Himalayan Countries*, FAO Fisheries Technical Paper, No. 431, FAO, Rome, pp. 47-58.

Thomas, D. H. L. (1996): "Fisheries Tenure in an African Floodplain Village and the Implications for Management", *Human Ecology*, Vol. 24, No. 3, pp. 287-313.

Viner, K. *et al.* (2006): "Development of Fisheries Co-management in Cambodia: A case study and its implications", *Discussion Series No. 2*, World Fish Center Contribution No. 1788, Malaysia.

Yaqoob, M. (2002): "Cold Water Fisheries of Pakistan", in Petr, T. and Swar, D.B. (eds.) *Cold Water Fisheries in the Trans-Himalayan Countries*, FAO Fisheries Technical Paper, No. 431, FAO, Rome, pp. 99-104.

Zaman, T. et al. (2006): "Present Status of Pond Fishery Resources and Livelihood of the Fish Farmers of Mohanpur Upazila in Rajshahi District", *University Journal of Zoology, Rajshahi University*, Vol. 25, pp. 31-35.

Zen, L.W. et al. (2002): "Technical Efficiency of the Driftnet and Payang Seine (Lampara) Fisheries in West Sumatra", Indonesia, *Asian Fisheries Science*, Vol. 15, pp. 97-106.

Chapter -3

Fisheries in India, North Eastern Region of India and Arunachal Pradesh

Introduction

There was a rapid increase in global income over the last few decades. In spite of rapid economic growth in many countries of the world, a good proportion of the global population continues to suffer from food insecurity and malnutrition. The figures of Food and Agricultural Organization (FAO) show that around 823 million people in developing countries were undernourished. There is also evidence that the number of people who remain vulnerable to food insecurity is considerably high (FAO, 2006). Therefore, the question arises whether it will be realistic to measure the developmental achievements in terms of physical output or not. There is consensus among the scholars that the health status of the people may be taken as the most accurate and dependable image of the development of the society.

Poor nutrition is an important outcome of food insecurity. Food insecurity causes poverty, vulnerability and livelihood insecurity but at the same time they are the consequences of these considerations. In fact, it is a vicious circle. In order to break this vicious circle the Government of India initiated a number of centrally sponsored schemes and central sector schemes at the State level. As a result, there is no doubt that macro level food self-sufficiency was achieved through increasing food production as well as public grain procurement and distribution. However, this has proved insufficient to ensure micro-level food security for the poor. The increase in food production and improved distribution system may be a necessary condition for achieving food security. For example, it is evident from recent studies that India needs to sustain agricultural growth rate of around 4 per cent in order to reduce food insecurity and poverty. In order to sustain this growth rate over the years there is a need for diversifying agricultural allied activities like fisheries.

Fishery, as a capable means of livelihood enhancement diversification has become an important topic of discussion and debate since the early nineties. As a result, the importance of small-scale fisheries to the livelihoods of rural populations and as a means of nexus of poverty and food insecurity in developing countries has gained momentum. However, it is necessary to make small-scale fisheries more efficient and, in some cases, less damaging to the associated cultural and resource assets (Misra, 2010). Statistics reveals that the global aquaculture is growing by around 3.2 per cent annually in the period 1961–2009 which is higher than the food production (FAO, 2012). FAO estimates that there are 38 million fish farmers across the globe and that 90 per cent are engaged in Small Scale Fisheries (SSF) activities (FAO, 2010). Although SSF are found both among the developed and developing countries, it is in developing countries that their contribution to food security and nutrition is more apparent. For example, in the Mekong Delta region of South East Vietnam, more than 15 million people were classified as small-scale fish farmers (Loc, V. T. T. *et al.*, 2010). A survey conducted by Water Resource Institute in 2000 revealed that 89 per cent of Philippine's low income small scale fisheries feed their families from the daily catches (World Bank, 2004).

Fisheries in India

Traditionally, fishing has been a major source of livelihood for inland fishing communities of India as well as a source of healthy food for the people. In fact, India has a vast potential for development of inland fisheries. India's inland fishery resources are vast and varied comprising of rivers, canals, reservoirs, lakes, flood plains, etc. The details are given in Table 3.1.

Table 3.1 shows that India's inland water resources consist of rivers and canals (1,95,210 km), reservoirs (0.29 million hectare), ponds and tanks (0.24 million hectare), lakes, flood plain and derelict water bodies (0.07 million hectare). In addition there were marine fishery resources which are shown in the following Table (Table 3.2).

Table 3.1: Inland Water Resources of India

Rivers and Canals (in km)	1,95,210
Reservoirs (in lakh ha.)	29.07
Tanks and Ponds (in lakh ha.)	24.14
Floodplain, Lakes and Derelict Water (in lakh ha.)	7.98
Total Water Bodies (in lakh ha.)	73.59

Source: Annual Report 2011-12, Department of Animal Husbandry, Dairying and Fisheries, Government of India.

Table 3.2: Marine Fishery Resources of India

Approx. Length of Coast Line (in km)	8118
Continental Shelf (in '000 sq. km)	530
Number of Landing Centres	1336
Number of Fishing Villages	3239

Source: Annual Report 2011-12, Department of Animal Husbandry, Dairying and Fisheries, Government of India.

Table 3.2 shows that marine fishery resources of India consist of approx. 8,118 km of length of coast lines, 5,30,000 sq. km of continental shelf, 1,336 landing centres and 3,289 fishing villages in the country. As a result, India is a major maritime State and an important aquaculture country in the world. With the third position in total fish production and a second in aquaculture (Appendix I), the country has high potential in this sector for rural development, domestic nutritional security, employment generation as well as export earnings. However, there was a structural change of production of fish in India. In 1960-61, marine

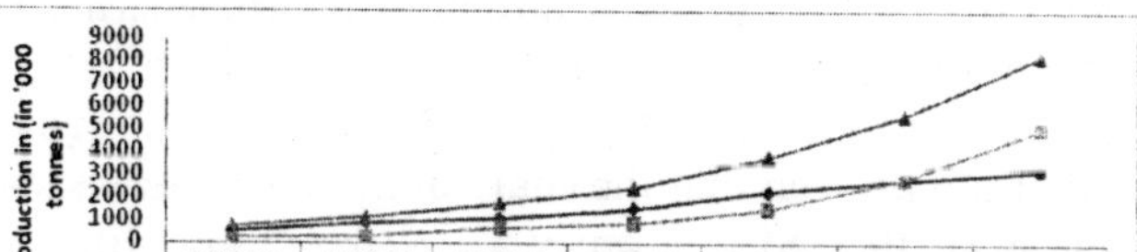

	1950-51	1960-61	1970-71	1980-81	1990-91	2000-01	2010-11
Marine	534	880	1086	1555	2300	2811	3220
Inland	218	280	670	887	1536	2845	5068
Total	752	1160	1756	2442	3836	5656	8288

Fig. 3.1: Fish Production in India during 1950-51 to 2010-11 (in '000 tonnes)

Sources: 1. Hand Book on Fisheries Statistics 2006, Government of India.

2. Annual Report 2011-12, Department of Animal Husbandry, Dairying and Fisheries, Government of India.

fisheries used to contribute 75.86 per cent of total fish production but its share was reduced to only 38.85 per cent in 2010-11. On the other hand, there was a significant increase in the contribution of inland fisheries to total fish production. The details are shown in the Fig. 3.1.

This paradigm shift from marine fisheries to inland fisheries in terms of production became clear during the last decade. More specifically, things began to change since the nineties. The increasing demand for fish products domestically and in international market, its potential to earn significant foreign exchange, stagnating marine fish production along with its associated crisis, availability of underutilized and unutilized water resources in inland region, etc., lead the policy makers to come out with certain interventions through passive and defensive measures, in the form of promotional and segmental policies. In recent years there has been an increasing realism among planners and policy makers that aquaculture has adequate potential and ample opportunities to provide employment and reduced poverty in rural areas by creating sustainable fishery based livelihood. As a result, India's contribution in global fish production appears significant. The details are shown in Table 3.3 and Figure 3.2.

Table 3.3 reflects that the world's fish production increased from19.76 million tonnes in 1950 to 140.48 million tonnes in 2004 (i.e., 7.1 times increase). On the other hand, India's fish production has increased to 6.09 million tonnes in 2004 from a mere 0.73 million tonnes in 1950 (i.e., 8.3 times increase). As a result, the share of India in global fish production increased from 2.6 per cent in 1965 to 4.33 per cent in 2004.

It shows that growth in fish production in India was at a faster rate than that of the world which was mainly due to increasing contribution from inland fisheries and aquaculture. From the Figure 3.2, it can be seen that the share of India's fisheries started increasing since 1980-81 and gained a sharp momentum in the mid-nineties. However, after 2004-05, India's contribution to global fisheries declined marginally which was mainly due to increasing contribution of some other developing countries.

In fact, fish production started increasing significantly from Sixth Five Year Plan onwards during which it attained the total increase of around 47.11 per cent (Government of India, 2006). Its

Table 3.3 : Fish Production in World and India during 1950 to 2004

(in '000 tonnes)

Year	*Fish Production*					
	World			*India*		
	Marine	*Inland*	*Total*	*Marine*	*Inland*	*Total*
1950	17521	2234	19755	520 (2.97)	210 (9.40)	730 (3.70)
1955	24968	3673	28641	596 (2.39)	243 (6.62)	839 (2.93)
1960	32665	4026	36691	880 (2.69)	282 (7.00)	1162 (3.17)
1965	46141	5088	51229	824 (1.79)	507 (9.96)	1331 (2.60)
1970	61277	6003	67280	1086 (1.77)	673 (11.21)	1759 (2.61)
1975	61481	6860	68341	1482 (2.41)	785 (11.44)	2267 (3.32)
1980	67953	7633	75586	1555 (2.29)	891 (11.67)	2446 (3.24)
1985	80888	10665	91553	1747 (2.16)	1092 (10.24)	2839 (3.10)
1991	84664	13597	98261	2390 (2.82)	1655 (12.17)	4045 (4.12)
1992	86329	14556	100885	2512 (2.91)	1720 (11.82)	4232 (4.19)
1993	88351	16126	104477	2676 (3.03)	1930 (11.97)	4606 (4.41)
1994	94659	17900	112559	2796 (2.95)	1989 (11.11)	4785 (4.25)
1995	96220	20191	116411	2754 (2.86)	2197 (10.88)	4951 (4.25)
1996	98038	22161	120199	2910 (2.97)	2321 (10.47)	5231 (4.35)
1997	98783	23759	122542	2949 (2.99)	2436 (10.25)	5385 (4.39)
1998	92593	25197	117790	2763 (2.98)	2512 (9.97)	5275 (4.48)
1999	99468	27183	126651	2848 (2.86)	2744 (10.09)	5592 (4.42)
2000	101831	28602	130433	2852 (2.80)	2837 (9.92)	5689 (4.36)
2001	101550	29452	131002	2930 (2.89)	2967 (10.07)	5897 (4.50)
2002	102953	30698	133651	3107 (3.02)	2817 (9.18)	5924 (4.43)
2003	101828	31359	133187	3107 (3.05)	2918 (9.31)	6025 (4.52)
2004	107390	33085	140475	2986 (2.78)	3102 (9.38)	6088 (4.33)

Note: Figures in the parentheses indicate the percentage of world fish production.
Source: Hand Book on Fisheries Statistics 2006, Government of India.

impressive growth continued during the subsequent planning period and post-liberalization era. Finally, an attempt was made to estimate the exponential growth rate of total fish production as well as inland and marine fish production separately as follows:

$\ln Y = 3.6 + 0.014t$

$R^2 = 0.979$, $\overline{R}^2 = 0.978$ and $n = 21$

Where Y is the total fish production of India, t is the time measured in years, with origin at 1990-91 and the period covered is 1990-91 to 2010-11 (Appendix II), number of observations is 21. The annual average exponential growth rate is 1.4 per cent which is significant at 0.01 per cent level. The same process can be followed for marine and inland fish production in India.

For inland fish production the equation is as follows:

$\ln Y = 3.19 + 0.025t$

$R^2 = 0.994,\ \overline{R}^2 = 0.994$ and $n = 21$

The average annual exponential growth rate for inland fish production was found to be 2.5 per cent with 0.01 per cent level of significance during the period of 1990-91 to 2010-11.

For marine fish production the equation is as follows:

$\ln Y = 3.404 + 0.004t$

$R^2 = 0.526,\ \overline{R}^2 = 0.501$ and $n = 21$

The average annual exponential growth rate for marine fish production was found to be 0.4 per cent with 0.01 per cent level of significance during the period of 1990-91 to 2010-11.

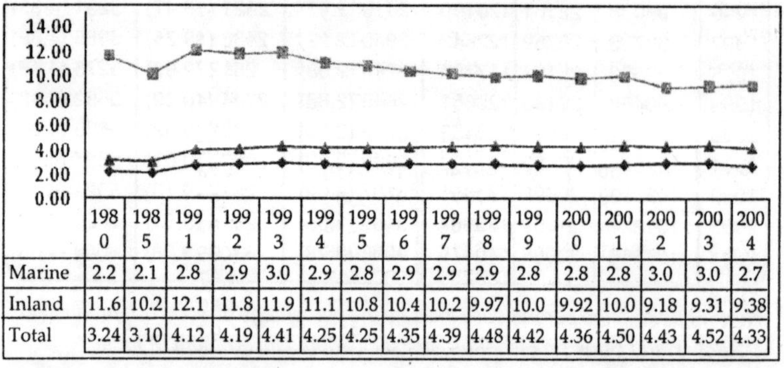

	1980	1985	1991	1992	1993	1994	1995	1996	1997	1998	1999	2000	2001	2002	2003	2004
Marine	2.2	2.1	2.8	2.9	3.0	2.9	2.8	2.9	2.9	2.9	2.8	2.8	2.8	3.0	3.0	2.7
Inland	11.6	10.2	12.1	11.8	11.9	11.1	10.8	10.4	10.2	9.97	10.0	9.92	10.0	9.18	9.31	9.38
Total	3.24	3.10	4.12	4.19	4.41	4.25	4.25	4.35	4.39	4.48	4.42	4.36	4.50	4.43	4.52	4.33

Fig. 3.2: India's Share in World Fish Production during 1980 to 2004 (in *percentage*)
Source: Hand Book on Fisheries Statistics 2006, Government of India.

Table 3.4 shows that, as a result of rapid growth of inland fish production, this fishery sector possessed higher growth rate than other food production sectors.

Thus, India's fisheries constituted an important sector of our national economy for various reasons. One of the important reasons is its increasing contribution to our Gross Domestic Product (GDP) which is given in Table 3.5 :

Table 3.4: Production (in million tonnes)and Growth Rate (in percentage) of Major Agricultural Commodities and Fisheries in India during 1949-50 to1998-99

(in million tonnes)

Year	*Rice*		*Wheat*		*Other Food grains*		*Fish*	
	Prod.	*G.R.*	*Prod.*	*G.R.*	*Prod.*	*G.R.*	*Prod.*	*G.R.*
1949-50	23.54	—	6.39	—	54.92	—	0.75	—
1979-80	42.33	79.82	31.83	398.12	109.70	99.75	2.34	212.00
1989-90	73.57	73.80	49.85	56.61	171.04	55.92	3.68	57.26
1998-99	85.99	16.88	70.78	41.99	203.04	18.71	5.26	42.93

Note: Prod. = Production and G.R. = Growth Rate

Source: Oxford Handbook of Agriculture in India, 2007.

Table 3.5: Contribution of Fishery Sector to India's GDP and Agricultural Sector during 1970-71 to 2010-11 (at current prices)

(in ₹ crore)

Year	*Fisheries*	*Agricultural Sector*	*GDP*	*Percentage Contribution of Fisheries to*	
				Agriculture	*GDP*
1970-71	245	16821	39708	1.46	0.62
1975-76	567	26651	71201	2.13	0.80
1980-81	921	42466	122427	2.17	0.75
1985-86	1974	69964	233799	2.82	0.84
1990-91	4556	135162	475604	3.37	0.96
1995-96	12729	312791	1103238	4.07	1.15
2000-01	21336	449746	1925415	4.74	1.11
2005-06	31699	637772	3390503	4.97	0.93
2006-07	35182	722984	3953276	4.87	0.89
2007-08	38931	836518	4582086	4.65	0.85
2008-09	44073	943204	5303567	4.67	0.83
2009-10	52363	1079365	6091485	4.85	0.86
2010-11	62594	1269888	7157412	4.93	0.87

Sources: 1. Hand Book on Fisheries Statistics 2006, Government of India.
2. Report of the Working Group on Fisheries for the Eleventh Five Year Plan, Government of India.

Table 3.5 shows that fishery's contribution to India's GDP was ₹245 crore in 1970-71 and increased to ₹62,594 crore (i.e., 255 times increase) in 2010-11. On the other hand, agricultural sector's contribution to India's GDP was ₹16,821 crore and it increased to ₹12,69,888 crore (i.e., 75 times increase) during the same period. It shows that fishery's contribution to India's GDP increased faster than that of agricultural sector. Although fishery's contribution to India's GDP remained constant in percentage term since India's GDP increased significantly during the post reform era. But fishery's contribution to agricultural sector in terms of GDP had an increasing trend. This rise in fish production was possible due to a quantum jump in inland fish production, especially pond aquaculture, which is growing at an average growth rate of 13.87 per cent.

Fisheries in the North Eastern Region of India

The North Eastern Region of India has vast untapped potential for fisheries in terms of many rivers, streams, floodplain wetlands, lakes, ponds and large areas under rice fish culture system. The rivers Brahmaputra and Barak form the principal drainage of North East India with its numerous tributaries flowing through the different States. The region has 20,875 km of rivers, 5.63 lakh hectares of water bodies as well as 2,760 hectares of paddy-cum-fish culture area. The details are given in Table 3.6.

Table 3.6: Inland Water Resources of North Eastern Region of India

	North Eastern Region (NER)	*India*	*NER's Contribution to India*
Rivers and Canals (in km)	20875	195210	10.69 %
Reservoirs (in lakh ha.)	0.33	29.07	1.14 %
Tanks and Ponds (in lakh ha.)	3.71	24.14	15.37 %
Floodplain, Lakes and Derelict Water (in lakh ha.)	1.59	7.98	19.92 %
Total Water Bodies (in lakh ha.)	5.63	73.59	7.65 %

Source: Annual Report 2011-12, Department of Animal Husbandry, Dairying and Fisheries, Government of India.

From Table 3.6 it is found that the region consists of only around 8 per cent of total geographical area of the country but it contains 9.58 per cent of rivers and canals, 19.92 per cent of flood plains lakes and derelict water and 15.37 per cent of tanks and ponds of the country. In fact, North East India is considered as one of the hot spots of freshwater fish biodiversity in the world. This water resource harbours 258 fish species belonging to 21 families and 76 genera (Mahanta *et al.*, 2010). The literature reveals that efforts were being made to assess the rice fish germplasm resources available in this region with respect to commercial utilization. With growing demand for consumption, aquarium and sports, it is necessary to evaluate potential species on the basis of different criteria. At this stage, assessment is only preliminary, since it is mainly based on the secondary data supplemented by interaction with experts and actual observation. This study reveals that accordingly to preliminary evaluation, out of 186 fish species 62 (33.33 per cent) were considered as only food fish followed by 53 (28.44 per cent) as only ornamental. The rest were food as well as ornamental (12.90 per cent), sports as well as ornamental (9.67 per cent), etc. (NEDFi Data Bank, 2007). So far economic value is concerned, it is evaluated that out of the 186 species, 34 fish species have market demand better than Indian major carp whereas 19 species have similar economic values. This indicates that there is great potential for fresh water fisheries in the States of North East India through culture of indigenous fish species. In addition to it, in this region of the country, the fish is traditionally raised along with paddy or rain fed low lands (both shallow and deep water). In many areas, irrigation fed rice fields have also been adapted locally by the farmers to include fish farming (Das, 2002). The traditional rice-fish production systems have an important socio-economic impact in the life of the farmers and fisheries in the region. As a result, during the last two decades, there was a rapid increase of fish production in North Eastern Region from 112.35 thousand tonnes in 1990-91 to 313.94 thousand tonnes in 2010-11. That means on an average the fish production increased around 10.08 tonnes annually during the period. The details are given in Table 3.7.

Table 3.7 shows that there is variation of fish production among the States of North East India. The two relatively plain States like Assam and Tripura jointly contributed 88.06 per cent of total fish production of the region during 2010-11. In fact, Assam's lone contribution to total fish production of the region was 72.38 per cent during 2010-11. Among the hilly States, the largest contribution was by Manipur (6.44 per cent) during 2010-11.

The average growth rate of fisheries of North Eastern Region as a whole was estimated as follows:

In Y=2.197+0.013t

Table 3.7: Fish Production in North Eastern Region of India during 1990-91 to 2010-11

(in '000 tonnes)

Year	*1990-91*	*1995-96*	*2000-01*	*2005-06*	*2010-11*
Arunachal Pradesh	1.25	1.85	2.60	2.75	3.04
Assam	76.00	155.06	158.62	188.00	227.24
Manipur	8.50	12.50	16.05	18.22	20.20
Meghalaya	1.52	3.58	4.97	4.12	4.56
Mizoram	2.95	2.50	3.15	3.75	2.90
Nagaland	0.83	3.00	5.20	5.50	6.59
Sikkim	0.10	0.15	0.14	0.15	0.18
Tripura	21.20	25.71	29.42	23.87	49.23
North Eastern Region (NER)	112.35	204.35	220.15	246.36	313.94
India	3835.89	4949.39	5655.34	6571.62	8294.68
NER's Contribution to India (%)	2.93	4.13	3.89	3.75	3.78

Sources: 1. Hand Book on Fisheries Statistics 2006, Government of India.
2. Annual Report 2011-12, Department of Animal Husbandry, Dairying and Fisheries, Government of India.

$R^2 = 0.791, \overline{R}^2 = 0.780$, and $n = 21$

Thus, we find that in the region fish production increased at an annual average exponential rate of 1.3 per cent during the last two decades which was marginally lower than that of India (1.4 per cent). However the contribution of fisheries to the region's Net State Domestic Product (NSDP) was relatively high than that of India and had an increasing trend. In fact, the fishery's contribution to the region's NSDP increased from 2.93 per cent in 1990-91 to 3.78 per cent in 2010-11. The contribution of fisheries and agriculture and allied sector to Net State Domestic Product among the various States of North East India in different years are summarised in Table 3.8 (A) and 3.8 (B).

From Table 3.8 (B) it is found that among the States of the region, Manipur's fishery's contribution to NSDP was the highest but it had a declining tendency. Except Nagaland, Sikkim and Tripura the share was lying in between 1 to 2 per cent in the other States of the region. However, the contribution of fishery to agriculture and allied sector of the region as a whole remained more than 5 per cent during the last decade.

Table 3.8 (A) : Contribution of Fisheries to Agriculture and Allied Activities and NSDP in North Eastern Region of India during 2004-05 to 2010-11 *(at current price)*

(in₹ lakh)

	Sector	*2004-05*	*2005-06*	*2006-07*	*2007-08*	*2008-09*	*2009-10*	*2010-11*
AP	Fisheries	1810	2158	2481	2949	3080	3300	3819
	Agricultural Sector	118658	124425	138429	158776	166071	199347	246200
	NSDP	318793	343947	376503	440735	519887	562068	763200
AS	Fisheries	69139	101172	128583	128814	137149	145103	157463
	Agricultural Sector	1262798	1563274	1584774	1712620	2101837	2500682	2833782
	NSDP	4718075	5243969	5703346	6234163	7176298	8169100	9249560
MN	Fisheries	10146	10495	11177	11920	12103	12264	12775
	Agricultural Sector	115476	127778	136363	147614	169326	190346	210134
	NSDP	460330	513793	550286	604907	661446	743640	822831
ML	Fisheries	3088	2948	2629	2368	2465	2551	2679
	Agricultural Sector	142961	152512	190912	196059	208386	235508	263198
	NSDP	584566	646053	770074	864191	1035212	1122856	1262307
MZ	Fisheries	2631	2691	2780	1839	1843	2328	NA
	Agricultural Sector	58905	60250	63405	74725	88848	115222	NA
	NSDP	239960	266427	294409	341053	415422	507800	NA
NL	Fisheries	2044	2318	2519	2621	3916	NA	NA
	Agricultural Sector	194249	202701	206328	209487	240639	NA	NA
	NSDP	542146	611627	672842	747715	862164	NA	NA

Table 3.8 (A) : *(Contd...)*

	Sector	*2004-05*	*2005-06*	*2006-07*	*2007-08*	*2008-09*	*2009-10*	*2010-11*
SK	Fisheries	68	79	90	101	107	133	156
	Agricultural Sector	28354	30604	32157	37570	43608	49231	56825
	NSDP	151083	173366	187098	213974	279586	414449	494258
TR	Fisheries	11924	13226	16091	22274	24662	27306	30233
	Agricultural Sector	213044	237353	242070	257717	267168	277088	287508
	NSDP	816969	904045	998061	1080809	1172254	1273387	1385365
NER	Fisheries	100850	135087	166350	172886	185325	NA	NA
	Agricultural Sector	2134445	2498897	2594438	2794568	3285883	NA	NA
	NSDP	7831922	8703227	9552619	10527547	12122269	NA	NA

Note: AP=Arunachal Pradesh, AS=Assam, MN=Manipur, ML=Meghalaya, MZ=Mizoram, NL=Nagaland, SK=Sikkim, TR=Tripura, NER= North Eastern Region and NSDP= Net State Domestic Product

Source: www.db.nedfi.com, assessed on 17th September, 2012.

Table 3.8 (B) : Contribution of Fisheries to Agriculture and Allied Activities and NSDP in North Eastern Region of India during 2004-05 to 2010-11 (at current prices)

(in percentage)

		2004-05	2005-06	2006-07	2007-08	2008-09	2009-10	2010-11
AP	1	1.53	1.73	1.79	1.86	1.85	1.66	1.55
	2	0.57	0.63	0.66	0.67	0.59	0.59	0.50
AS	1	5.48	6.47	8.11	7.52	6.53	5.80	5.56
	2	1.47	1.93	2.25	2.07	1.91	1.78	1.70
MN	1	8.79	8.21	8.20	8.08	7.15	6.44	6.08
	2	2.20	2.04	2.03	1.97	1.83	1.65	1.55
ML	1	2.16	1.93	1.38	1.21	1.18	1.08	1.02
	2	0.53	0.46	0.34	0.27	0.24	0.23	0.21
MZ	1	4.47	4.47	4.38	2.46	2.07	2.02	NA
	2	1.10	1.01	0.94	0.54	0.44	0.46	NA
NL	1	1.05	1.14	1.22	1.25	1.63	NA	NA
	2	0.38	0.38	0.37	0.35	0.45	NA	NA
SK	1	0.24	0.26	0.28	0.27	0.25	0.27	0.27
	2	0.05	0.05	0.05	0.05	0.04	0.03	0.03
TR	1	5.60	5.57	6.65	8.64	9.23	9.85	10.52
	2	1.46	1.46	1.61	2.06	2.10	2.14	2.18
NER	1	4.72	5.41	6.41	6.19	5.64	NA	NA
	2	1.29	1.55	1.74	1.64	1.53	NA	NA

Note: AP=Arunachal Pradesh, AS=Assam, MN=Manipur, ML=Meghalaya, MZ=Mizoram, NL=Nagaland, SK=Sikkim, TR= Tripura, NER= North Eastern Region, 1= Contribution of Fisheries to Agricultural Sector, and 2= Contribution of Fisheries to Net State Domestic Product.

Source: www.db.nedfi.com, assessed on 17th September, 2012.

Status of Fisheries in Arunachal Pradesh

Arunachal Pradesh, our study area, is located in the extreme north eastern corner of India. The State is well endowed for inland water fisheries. It is situated in the monsoon belt. It received an average annual rainfall of around 2721.80 mm (Government of Arunachal Pradesh, 2011). The State has extensive inland water resources in the form of rivers, hill streams, wetlands, lakes, ponds, etc. The details are given in Table 3.9.

Table 3.9: Inland Water Resources of Arunachal Pradesh

	Arunachal Pradesh	*North Eastern Region (NER)*	*Arunachal's Contribution to NER (in per cent)*
Rivers and Canals (in km)	2000	20875	9.58
Reservoirs (in lakh ha.)	0.00	0.33	0.00
Tanks and Ponds (in lakh ha.)	2.76	3.71	74.39
Floodplain, Lakes and Derelict Water (in lakh ha.)	0.42	1.59	26.42
Total Water Bodies (in lakh ha.)	3.18	5.63	56.48
Total Geographical Area (in sq. km.)	83,743	2,62,179	31.94

Sources: 1. Annual Report 2011-12, Department of Animal Husbandry, Dairying and Fisheries, Government of India.
2. Basic Statistics of North Eastern Region, 2006.

Table 3.9 shows that Arunachal Pradesh consists of around 31.94 per cent of the total geographical area of the North Eastern Region of India but it contains 26.42 per cent of flood plain, lakes and derelict water, 74.39 per cent of tanks and ponds and 56.48 per cent of total water bodies of the region. Thus, the State has enormous potential for development of fisheries in the region. In fact, fish, from time immemorial, has been an important dietary food of the people of the State. In addition, paddy-cum-fish cultivation is an important component of fisheries in general and culture fisheries in particular of the State. The best example of the paddy-cum-fish culture of the State is the Apatani plateau of Lower Subansiri district. There was not much reliable data regarding the extent of area of paddy-cum-fish cultivation in the State. According to one study (Das, 2002) the rice fish culture area consisted of around 53.48 per cent of cultured fisheries area. The details are given in Table 3.10.

Table 3.10: Developed Paddy-*cum*-Fish Culture Area and Total Fish Culture Area in Arunachal Pradesh

(in ha.)

Districts	*Paddy-cum-Fish Culture Area*	*Total Fish Culture Area*
Tawang	50.00 (5.80)	66.23 (4.11)
West Kameng	75.00 (8.70)	114.70 (7.12)
East Kameng	15.00 (1.74)	39.18 (2.43)
Lower Subansiri	547.00 (63.46)	626.76 (38.89)
Papumpare	10.00 (1.16)	136.19 (8.45)
Upper Subansiri	69.00 (8.00)	123.19 (7.64)
West Siang	40.00 (4.64)	87.14 (5.41)
East Siang	22.00 (2.55)	72.22 (4.48)
Upper Siang	17.00 (1.97)	42.25 (2.62)
Dibang Valley	0.00 (0.00)	38.98 (2.42)
Lohit	7.00 (0.81)	148.97 (9.24)
Tirap	10.00 (1.16)	45.22 (2.81)
Changlang	0.00 (0.00)	70.70 (4.39)
Arunachal Pradesh	862.00 (53.48)*	1611.73

*Note:*Figures in the parentheses indicate the percentage of total.

* Figure indicates percentage of total culture fish area.

Source: Das, 2002.

Table 3.10 shows that lower Subansiri district alone (63.46 per cent) had the highest percentage of paddy-cum-fish cultivation among all the districts of Arunachal Pradesh. The contribution of other districts was insignificant. In fact, recently rice-cum-fish-cum duck cultivation is growing popular in Lohit district (*The Arunachal Times*, 14th September, 2012). According to another estimate (Moda, 2005) paddy field consisted of 40.04 per cent of total fisheries in the State. The details are given in Table 3.11 and Figure 3.3.

Table 3.11 shows that among the various sources ponds and tanks (47.36 per cent) dominated the utilization of fisheries resources in Arunachal Pradesh. The State which is very rich in lakes and various natural water bodies are hardly exploited for fishery purposes. Recently, efforts were initiated by the State

Table 3.11: Utilization Status of Fishery Resources of Arunachal Pradesh, 2004

Types of resources	*Estimated (in ha.)*	*Utilization (in ha.)*	*Utilization as percentage of Estimated*
Ponds and Tanks	2200	1042	47.36
Beels and Lakes	2000	107	5.35
Paddy Fields	2800	1121	40.04
Rivers and Streams	2000	100	5.00

Source: Moda, 2005

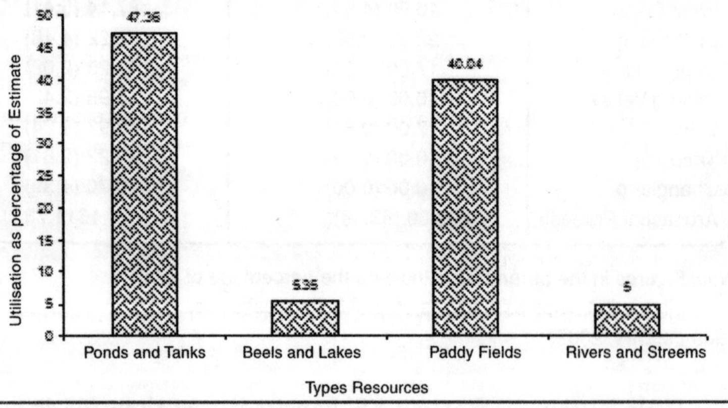

Source: Moda, 2005.

Fig. 3.3: Utilization Status of Fishery Resources of Arunachal Pradesh, 2004 *(in per cent).*

Government to raise chocolate mahseer and common carp for Mehao Lake in Lower Dibang Valley district and the result is very encouraging (Das, Sarma and Mahanta, 2010). There is no proper documentation of fisheries in the State. A decade back Nath and Dey (2000) revealed that 131 species of fishes were available in the State. At this stage assessment is only preliminary since it is mainly based on the secondary data supplemented by interaction with experts and actual observation. The problem is that fish intake of the people of the State is dependent on the nature of fisheries in the local water bodies. It should be noted that in Arunachal earlier the fishery practices was basically capture fishing, i.e., direct fishing from the wild. The people in general indiscriminately exploited whatever species were available in the drainage systems as their food resources (Das, Sarma and Mahanta, 2010).

Trends of Production of Fishes in Arunachal Pradesh

The fisheries programme was first initiated in the year 1958-59 in a very modest scale. However, with the passage of time and expansion of fisheries development activities, pisciculture has taken a firm root in the State. The people are presently looking forward to fisheries as a means of additional income and seeking more and more Government intervention for this purpose. This is attributed by the fact that the people are basically farmers taking fishery as a subsidiary occupation and no 'fisherman' exists by caste in the State (NEDFi Data Bank, 2007). In fact, the problems of flash flood, underutilization of aquatic resources, unscientific methods of culture and low level of people's participation are some of the important factors in lowering the production up to a minimum level. On the other hand it was found that per capita consumption of fish was one of the highest among the States of North East India, i.e., 0.704 kg/person/month in rural area and 0.799 kg/person/month in urban area next to Tripura (Appendix III). Thus it appears that there is a gap between production and consumption of fishes. However, there was a steady increase in production of fish since the nineties. The details are shown in Figure (Figure 3.4).

Figure 3.4 shows that fish production in Arunachal Pradesh increased from 1250 tonnes in 1990-91 to 3040 tonnes in 2010-11 (i.e., 2.4 times). An attempt was made to estimate the exponential growth of fish production during 1990-91 to 2010-11 is as follows:

$$\ln Y = 3.171 + 0.017t$$

$$R^2 = 0.859,\ \overline{R}^2 = 0.851 \text{ and } n = 21$$

Where Y is the total fish production of Arunachal Pradesh, t is the time measured in years, with origin at 1990-91 and the period

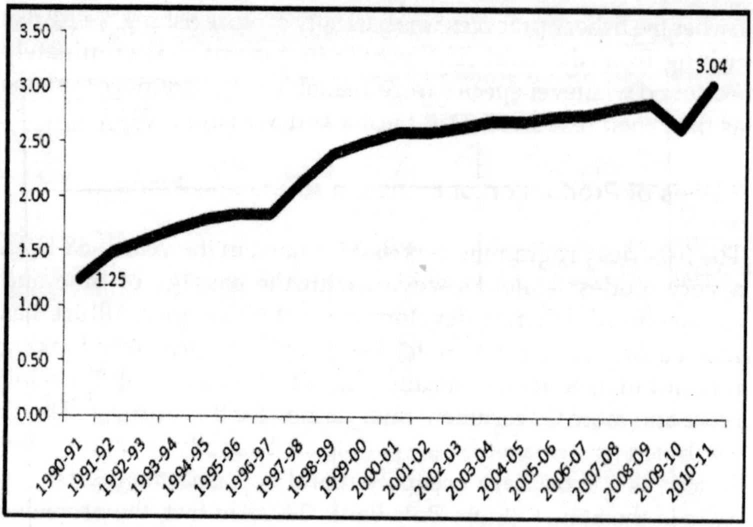

Source: Department of Fisheries, Government of Arunachal Pradesh, Itanagar.

Fig. 3.4: Fish Production in Arunachal Pradesh during 1990-91 to 2010-11 *(in '000 tonnes)*

covered is 1990-91 to 2010-11, with 21 observations (value of *n*). The average annual exponential growth rate was found to be 1.7 per cent which is significant at 0.01 per cent level. Thus, the production of fish in Arunachal Pradesh grew at an average rate of 1.7 per cent during 1990-91 to 2010-11 which is higher than that of the North Eastern Region as a whole (1.3 per cent). This increase in the production of fish was basically due to the increase in area under pisciculture. Table 3.12 shows that the area under pisciculture increased by 1.58 times whereas, the productivity of fish increased by 1.43 during the period of 1997-98 to 2010-11.

However, this estimate probably underestimated the actual production from riverine captured due to lack of actual data. The catches were accounted from ponds and tanks, beels and lakes and paddy fields. The rest of the fishes were still unexploited, except traditional fishing by the local people. Practically, culture fishes of Indian major carps and exotic carps contributed 66.53 per cent of total production of State. The harvest of other like fishes including Murrells and Catfishes from developed area contributed 15.45 per cent of total production (Das, 2005). Therefore, there is

Table 3.12: Area under Paddy-*cum*-Fish Culture and Production of Fish in Arunachal Pradesh during 1997-98 to 2010-11

Year	*Area under Paddy-cum-Fish Culture (in ha.)*	*Change (in per cent)*	*Production of Fish (in '000 tonnes)*	*Change (in per cent)*
1997-98	872	—	2.13	—
1998-99	902	3.44	2.40	12.68
1999-00	967	7.21	2.50	4.17
2000-01	1031	6.62	2.60	4.00
2001-02	1071	3.88	2.60	0.00
2002-03	1121	4.67	2.65	1.92
2003-04	1171	4.46	2.70	1.89
2004-05	1171	0.00	2.70	0.00
2005-06	1171	0.00	2.75	1.85
2006-07	1200	2.48	2.77	0.73
2007-08	1305	8.75	2.83	2.17
2008-09	1325	1.53	2.88	1.77
2009-10	1345	1.51	2.65	–7.99
2010-11	1375	2.30	3.04	14.72

Source: Department of Fisheries, Government of Arunachal Pradesh, Itanagar.

considerable scope for expansion of fish production in the State. The major part of fishery resources remained unutilized and underutilized. As a result the contribution of fisheries to NSDP remained less than 1 per cent (except 1991-92) during the last three decades (Table 3.13).

There is significant inter-district variation of production of fishes in Arunachal Pradesh. The details are shown in Figure 3.5.

From Figure 3.5 it is found that Lohit district (13.22 per cent) topped the production of fishes followed by Changlang (9.26 per cent). It is clear that the fish production is more in relatively foothills districts adjoining Assam borders. On the other hand, the fish production is less in hilly districts of the State in spite of the fact that there is so much scope for development of cold water fisheries in those hilly districts. The only exception was Lower Subansiri district where traditional paddy-cum-fish cultivation was very popular among the *Apatani* tribe of Ziro valley of Lower Subansiri district.

Table 3.13: Contribution of Fishery Sector to the Agriculture and Allied Activities and Total NSDP of Arunachal Pradesh during 1981-82 to 2011-12

(in ₹ lakh)

Year	*Fisheries*	*Agricultural Sector*	*Net State Domestic Product (NDSP)*	*Contribution of Fisheries to*	
				Agriculture and Allied Activities (in per cent)	*NSDP (in per cent)*
1981-82	8	6780	13118	0.12	0.06
1986-87	124	14948	28000	0.83	0.44
1991-92	634	25833	57236	2.46	1.11
1996-97	898	47106	108271	1.91	0.83
2001-02	1510	61223	198612	2.47	0.76
2002-03	1494	62744	195432	2.39	0.76
2003-04	1501	67522	223669	2.33	0.67
2004-05	1810	118658	318793	1.53	0.57
2005-06	2158	124425	343947	1.74	0.63
2006-07	2481	138429	376503	1.80	0.66
2007-08	2949	158776	440735	1.86	0.67
2008-09	3080	166071	519887	1.86	0.60
2009-10	3300	199347	652068	1.66	0.51
2010-11	3819	246200	763200	1.56	0.50
2011-12	4343	284700	869115	1.53	0.50

Source: Estimates of State Domestic Product of Arunachal Pradesh, 1998, 2004 and 2006, Government of Arunachal Pradesh.

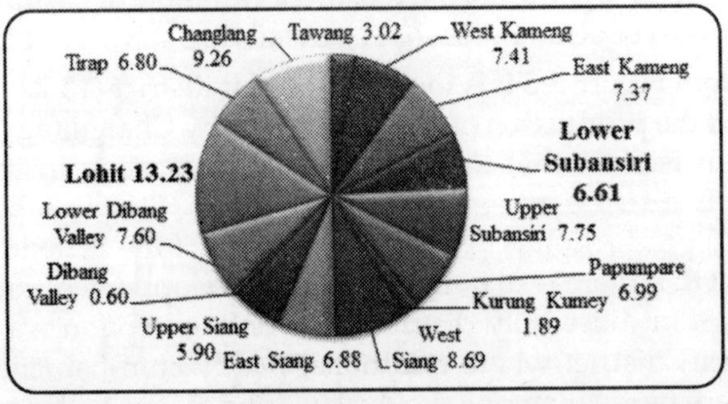

Source: Directorate of Fisheries, Government of Arunachal Pradesh.

Fig. 3.5 : District-wise Composition of Fish Production in Arunachal Pradesh, 2009 *(in per cent)*

Keeping in view the above facts, two districts namely Lohit, a relatively plain district and Lower Subansiri, a relatively hilly district were selected for an in-depth study of fisheries. The details were analysed in subsequent chapters based on the primary data.

References

Arunachal Times (2012): *The Arunachal Times*, 14th September, 2012 Issue, Itanagar. (www.arunachaltimes.in)

Das, D. N. (2002): "Fish Farming in Rice Environments of North Eastern India", *Aquaculture Asia*, Vol. VII, No. 2, pp. 43-47.

Das, D. N. (2005): "Utilisation of Fishery Resources in Arunachal Pradesh, India: An Overview of Socio-economic Dimension", in Tyagi, B. C. *et al.* (eds.), *Coldwater Fisheries Research and Development in North East Region of India*, National Research Centre on Coldwater Fisheries, Nainital, pp. 25-36.

Das, D. N. *et al.* (2010): "Scope for mountain fishery based eco-tourism in Arunachal Pradesh: Potential and recommendations", in Mahanta, P. C. and D. Sarma (eds.), *Coldwater Fisheries Management*, Directorate of Coldwater Fisheries Research, Nainital, pp. 285-296.

FAO (2006): *The State of World Fisheries and Aquaculture*, FAO, UN, Rome.

FAO (2010): *The State of World Fisheries and Aquaculture*, FAO, UN, Rome.

FAO (2012): *The State of World Fisheries and Aquaculture*, FAO, UN, Rome.

Government of Arunachal Pradesh (2011): *Statistical Abstract of Arunachal Pradesh*, Directorate of Economics and Statistics, Itanagar.

Government of Arunachal Pradesh (1998): *Estimates of State Domestic Product of Arunachal Pradesh 1998*, Directorate of Economics and Statistics, Itanagar.

Government of Arunachal Pradesh (2004): *Estimates of State Domestic Product of Arunachal Pradesh 2004*, Directorate of Economics and Statistics, Itanagar.

Government of Arunachal Pradesh (2006): *Estimates of State Domestic Product of Arunachal Pradesh 2006*, Directorate of Economics and Statistics, Itanagar.

Government of India (2006): *Basic Statistics of North Eastern Region 2006*, North Eastern Council, Shillong.

Government of India (2007): *Handbook on Fisheries in India 2006*, Department of Animal Husbandry, Dairying & Fisheries, Ministry of Agriculture, New Delhi.

Government of India (2012): *Annual Report 2011-12*, Department of Animal Husbandry, Dairying & Fisheries, Ministry of Agriculture, New Delhi.

Government of India (2006): *Report of the Working Group on Development and Management of Fisheries and Aquaculture for the XI Five Year Plan*, Planning Commission, New Delhi.

http://db.nedfi.com/

Loc, V. T. T. *et al.* (2010): "High and low value fish chains in the Mekong Delta: Challenges for Livelihoods and Governance", *Environ Dev Sustain*, Vol. 12, pp. 889–908.

Mahanta, P. C. *et al.* (2010): "Fishery Resources and Status of Fish Culture in Upland Waters of Arunachal Pradesh, India", in Mahanta, P. C. and D. Sarma (eds.), *Coldwater Fisheries Management*, Directorate of Coldwater Fisheries Research, Nainital, pp. 97-110.

Misra, S. R. (2012): *Sustainable Rural Livelihood Systems: The Case for India's Inland Fisheries Sector*, Concept Publishing Company (P) Ltd., New Delhi.

Moda, T. (2005): "Status Paper on Fisheries of Arunachal Pradesh", in Tyagi, B. C. et al. (eds.), *Coldwater Fisheries Research and Development in North East Region of India*, National Research Centre on Coldwater Fisheries, Nainital, pp.139-144.

Nath, P. and S.C. Dey (2000), *Fish and Fisheries of North Eastern India: Volume-I Arunachal Pradesh*, Narendra Publishers, New Delhi.

NEDFi (2007): *NEDFi Databank Quarterly*, Quarterly Journal on North Eastern States Economy Sericulture, Fisheries and Animal Husbandry, Vol. 5, Iss. II, III, and IV.

Ray, S. (ed.) (2011): *Handbook of Agriculture in India*, Oxford University Press, New Delhi.

World Bank (2004): Socio-Cultural Aspects of Developing Small Scale Fisheries, Vol. 73.

Chapter - 4

Socio-economic Characteristics, Livelihood Linkages of Surveyed Fish Farmers and Operational Features of Sampled Ponds

Introduction

The analysis of the secondary data undertaken in the preceding chapter has offered valuable insights into the trends, growth of production of fishes of India, in general, and North East India and Arunachal Pradesh in particular. However, there are many aspects of fishery in the State like operational features, livelihood linkages about which little is known from the secondary sources. Therefore, keeping in view the objectives of the study, a field survey covering two districts namely Lohit and Lower Subansiri from two different agro-climatic zones were selected. The present chapter proceeds to a detailed discussion of socio-economic characteristics, livelihood linkages, etc., of surveyed fish farmers as well as the operational features of sampled ponds in the study area.

Brief Description of Surveyed Districts

Lohit District

The present study was undertaken in Lohit district of Arunachal Pradesh which is located in the eastern Himalayan range with agriculture as the predominant occupation. Lohit is located in the eastern corner of the State and covers a geographical area of 5,212 sq. km. (6.22 per cent of total geographical area of the State) with a population of 1,45,538 persons (10.53 per cent of total population of the State) as per provisional population census, 2011. The district

of the State) as per provisional population census, 2011. The district derived its name from Lohit River, a tributary of the Brahmaputra that flows through the district. There were a number of administrative changes before it came into existence as the present Lohit district.

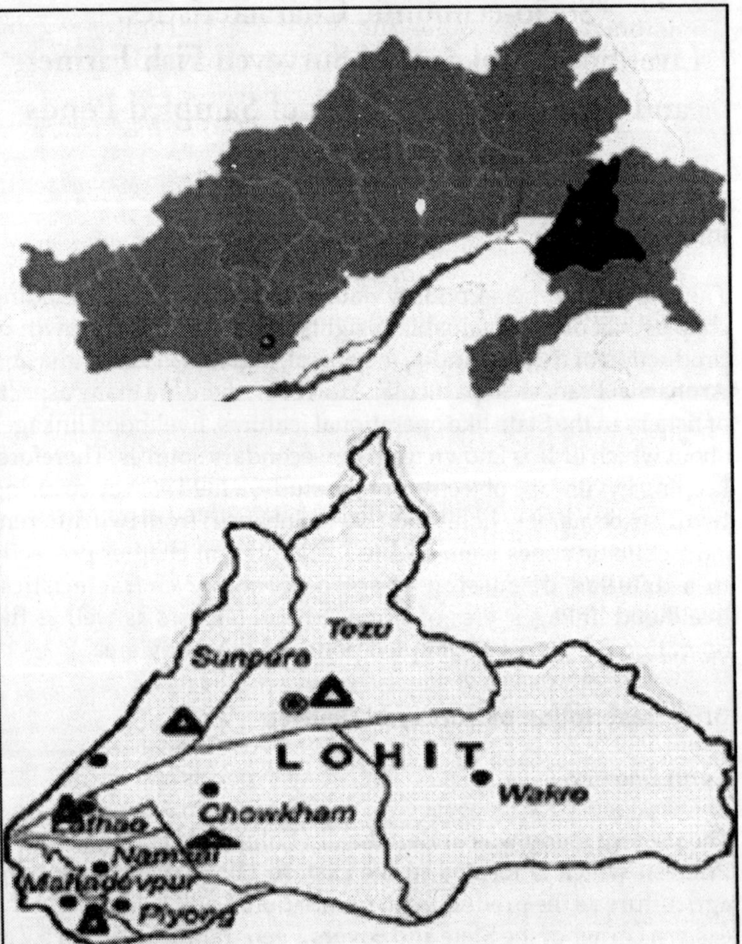

Map 4.1: Location Map of Lohit District showing the Surveyed Area

Note: Triangle ( ) in the map shows surveyed area.

when it became a part of the Eastern Section. In 1919, the Central and Eastern Sections were renamed as Sadia Frontier Tract which was later divided into two administrative units as the *Abor* Hills district and the *Mishmi* Hills district. In 1951, the plains of the *Mishmi* Hills district were transferred to Assam. In 1952, headquarters of the *Mishmi* Hills district was shifted to Tezu. In 1954, as the administrative nomenclature of the territory was changed from North Eastern Frontier Tract to North East Frontier Agency, the *Mishmi* Hills district was renamed as the Lohit Frontier Division. In 1965 under the North East Frontier Agency (Administrative) Regulation 1965, the Lohit Frontier Division came to be known as Lohit district. After Arunachal Pradesh became the Union Territory a number of administrative changes took place and as a result Lohit district was divided into two districts namely Lohit district and Dibang Valley district in June, 1980 under the Arunachal Pradesh Reorganization of Districts Act 1982. Further, Lohit district was bifurcated into two districts namely Lohit district and Anjaw district in February 2004. The study deals with the present Lohit district.

The economy of Lohit is basically agrarian contributing 28.47 per cent of Net District Domestic Product (NDDP) of the district. Apart from agriculture, people are also involved in services sector, rearing livestock, fisheries, etc. In fact, Lohit is the largest producer of fishes in the State (around 13.23 per cent of the total production of the State). In NDDP also, fisheries contributed around 1.86 per cent which is much higher than that of State average (0.75 per cent). An overview of socio-economic data of Lohit district can be observed from Table 4.1.

It should be noted that fishing in ponds and lakes are rarely known to indigenous tribes of the district. Traditionally, people do not practice fishing in the ponds and natural lakes. So, fishing in ponds and natural lakes was not a traditional practice. But presently people are practicing fishing in ponds and natural lakes as an economic activity.

The *Digaru Mishmis,* the *Khamptis* and the *Singphos* mainly inhabit Lohit district. The *Mishmis,* like most of the tribes of Arunachal Pradesh, practiced shifting cultivation. However, the *Khamptis* and *Singphos* are a few tribes of Arunachal Pradesh who practiced wet rice cultivation. The *Mishmi* tribe still has community

Table 4.1: Socio-economic Data of Lohit District

Geographical Area		5,212 *sq.km.*
Total Population		1,45,538
Literacy Rate	Male	77.25
	Female	61.62
	Total	69.88
Sex Ratio *(females per 1000 males)*		901
Density of Population		28 persons/sq.km.
Percentage of Villages Electrified		97.00 *per cent*
District Domestic Product *(at current Price 2007-08)*		₹42,612 *lakh*
Per Capita Income *(at current Price 2007-08)*		₹27,368

Sources: 1. Census of India, 2011.
2. Statistical Abstract of Arunachal Pradesh, 2012.

ownership of land. However, the *Khamptis* and *Singphos* have individual ownership of land. So, far as the water bodies are concerned, all the tribes had the community ownership known as village or clan ponds. They used to conduct community fishing during winter season and festival time (Choudhury *et al.*, 2008). Individual fishing is done whenever they wish and their time permits. In other words it is a leisure activity. However, now-a-days it is found that most of the water bodies and ponds of the district have individual ownership. It is interesting to observe that they have started fishing as a commercial activity.

Lower Subansiri District

The present study was also undertaken in Lower Subansiri district of Arunachal Pradesh which is located in the eastern Himalayan range with agriculture as the predominant occupation. Lower Subansiri is located in western corner of the State and covers a geographical area of 3,508 sq. km. (4.19 per cent of total geographical area of the State) with a population of 82,889 persons as per provisional population census, 2011.

The district derived its name from Subansiri River, very famous for its gold dust, a tributary of the mighty Brahmaputra, which flows through Raga circle of this district. Till 1914, the district was a part of Lakhimpur district of Assam. By the Government of India Notification of 1914, the area covered by this

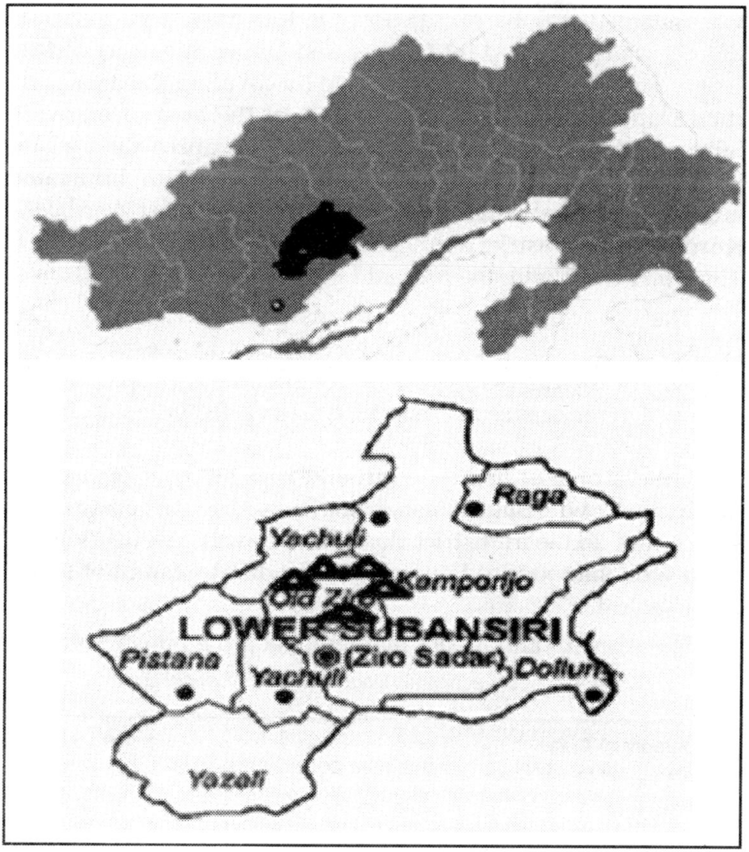

Map 4.2: Location Map of Lower Subansiri District showing the Surveyed Area
Note: Triangle ( ) in the map shows surveyed area.

Government of India Notification of 1914, the area covered by this district became a part of Lakhimpur Frontier Tract of the North East Frontier Tract. In March 1919, the Lakhimpur Frontier Tract along with Western sector was renamed as the Balipara Frontier Tract. In 1946, the district area was curved out of the Balipara Frontier Tract in the name of Subansiri Area with its Headquarters at North Lakhimpur. In 1954, Subansiri Area was renamed as the Subansiri Frontier Division and its Headquarters was later transferred to Ziro. On 1st September, 1965, the Ministry of Home Affairs took over the Administrative charge of NEFA from the was renamed as Subansiri district. On 13th May, 1980, Subansiri district was bifurcated into Lower and Upper Subansiri district. Upper Subansiri district was formed by covering the area of the then Daporijo Sub-Division and rest of the area of erstwhile Subansiri district was placed under Lower Subansiri. On the 22nd September, 1992, Lower Subansiri district was again bifurcated, and Papumpare district was formed. Finally, on 1st April, 2001 Kurung Kumey district was created from Lower Subansiri district. The study deals with the present Lower Subansiri district.

The economy of Lower Subansiri is basically agrarian contributing 35.70 per cent of Net District Domestic Product (NDDP) of the district. Apart from agriculture, people are also involved in services sector, rearing livestock, fisheries, etc. In fact, Lower Subansiri is one of the largest producers of fishes among the hill districts of the State (around 6.61 per cent of the total production of the State). Also, fisheries contributed around 0.60 per cent of the total district domestic product. An overview of socio-economic data of Lower Subansiri district can be observed from Table 4.2.

The *Apatanis* and *Nyshis* mainly inhabit the Lower Subansiri

Table 4.2: Socio-economic Data of Lower Subansiri District

Geographical Area		3,508 *sq.km.*
Total Population		82,839
Literacy Rate	Male	82.40
	Female	70.10
	Total	76.33
Sex Ratio *(females per 1000 males)*		975
Density of Population		24 persons/sq.km.
Percentage of Villages Electrified		81.70 *per cent*
District Domestic Product *(at current Price 2007-08)*		₹28,074 *lakh*
Per Capita Income *(at current Price 2007-08)*		₹26,886

Sources: 1. Census of India, 2011.
2. Statistical Abstract of Arunachal Pradesh 2012.

district. The *Apatani* practices aquaculture along with rice farming on their own their paddy field. Paddy-cum-fish culture in the valley is a unique practice in the State where fish and rice are raised together.

Integrating aquaculture with agriculture assures higher productivity and year round employment opportunities for farmers. The plots utilized for rice-cum-fish culture is mainly based on organic fertilization with varieties of animals excreta such as poultry dropping, pig excreta, cow dung and wastes of plants such as rice husks, waste product of local beer and ashes from household, and the remains of burnt straws after the harvest is over.

Table 4.3: Fish Farmer's Household Surveyed as per District, Block and Village

Sample Districts	*Sample Blocks Locality*	*Sample Villages/ Farmer Households*	*Surveyed Fish*
Lohit	Sunpura	Yeling	10
Lohit	Sunpura	Jaco	10
Lohit	Tezu	Khoroliang	10
Lohit	Tezu	Tafragram	10
Lohit	Namsai-Chongkham	Jona-I	10
Lohit	Namsai-Chongkham	Jona-II	10
Lohit	Namsai-Chongkham	Jona-III	20
Lohit	Namsai-Chongkham	Jona-IV	20
Lohit	Namsai-Chongkham	Nanang Khamyang-I	10
Lohit	Namsai-Chongkham	Nanang Khamgyang-II	10
Lohit	Namsai-Chongkham	Deo Beel-I	20
Lohit	Lekhang	Mahadevpur-I	20
Lohit	Lekhang	Mahadevpur-II	20
Lohit	Lekhang	Eraloni	20
Lower Subansiri	Ziro-I	Bulla	20
Lower Subansiri	Ziro-I	Hari	20
Lower Subansiri	Ziro-I	Hija	20
Lower Subansiri	Ziro-I	Hong	20
Lower Subansiri	Ziro-I	Mudang Tage	10
Lower Subansiri	Ziro-I	Dutta	10

Source: Field Survey, 2010-12.

The survey was undertaken in both the districts where fish

farming activities were carried on a large scale. The surveyed districts, blocks and villages were given in Table 4.3. It should be noted that twenty-fish farmer households were selected from those villages where fish farming is carried out comparatively in large scale and ten fish farmer households were selected from those villages where fish farming is done comparatively in small scale.

Socio-economic Characteristics of Fish Farmers Surveyed

Ponds fish production depends upon various variables used, the method of production practices (traditional or modern), type and size of the ponds and water bodies, experience in fish farming and also upon various socio-economic conditions of the fish farmers. The socio-economic characteristics of the fish farmers influence the extent of utilization of their ponds and water bodies significantly. So, in this section, an attempt was made to examine the socio-economic characteristics of fish farmers surveyed.

Fish farmer under study were grouped into three age category, i.e., (a) below 30 years, (b) 30 to 50 years, and (c) above 50 years. The details were given in Table 4.4.

Table 4.4: Age-wise Distribution of Fish Farmers in the Surveyed Districts *(in years)*

Districts	*Distribution of Age*			*Average Age of Household Heads*
	Below 30 years	*30 to 50 years*	*Above 50 years*	
Lohit	15 (7.50)	120 (60.00)	65 (32.50)	49
Lower Subansiri	9 (9.00)	63 (63.00)	28 (28.00)	42
Total	24 (8.00)	183 (61.00)	93 (31.00)	47

Note: Figures in parentheses indicate the respective percentages of total.
Source: Field Survey, 2010-12.

Table 4.4 shows that in both the districts more than 60 per cent of the surveyed fish farmers belonged to matured age category, i.e., 30-50 years. And 31 per cent belong to old age category, i.e., more than 50 years, only 8 per cent of surveyed fish farmers were young. It was observed that in Lohit district the average age of surveyed fish farmers was found to be higher, i.e., 49 years than that of Lower Subansiri district (42 years). It may be due to the fact that in Lohit district, a good number of ponds were found to be relatively large and matured farmers were found operating large size ponds since they had long experience and more managerial skill in fish production.

The education level of fish farmers were analysed since it affects the knowledge level, exposure to the production technology, marketing practices as well as capacity of absorption of improved technology. In order to examine the educational level of the fish farmers under study they are divided into five groups namely; (a) illiterates, (b) primary, (c) secondary, (d) higher secondary, and (e) Graduation and above. The details are given in Table 4.5.

Table 4.5: Educational Status of Fish Farmers Surveyed

Districts	*Illiterates*	*Primary*	*Secondary*	*Higher Secondary*	*Graduation and above*	*Total*
Lohit	79 (39.50)	45 (22.50)	36 (18.00)	27 (13.50)	13 (6.50)	200
Lower Subansiri	25 (25.00)	31 (31.00)	15 (15.00)	16 (16.00)	12 (12.00)	100
Total	104 (34.67)	76 (25.33)	51 (17.00)	43 (14.33)	25 (8.33)	300

Note: Figures in parentheses indicate the respective percentages of total.

Source: Field Survey, 2010-12.

From Table 4.5 it is clear that the overall education level of surveyed fish farmers were very low. Most of the surveyed fish farmers were illiterates (34.67 per cent). The number of illiterate surveyed fish farmers in case of Lohit district (39.5 per cent) was higher than that of Lower Subansiri district (25 per cent). It was also observed that only 8.33 per cent of the surveyed fish farmers were graduate and above.

The fish farmer's family size was examined to have an idea about the supply of human labours for fishing activities. A comparatively large family is expected to take care of fishing activity through family labour. The fish farmers family was divided into three categories according to number of family members, i.e., (a) small (less than 5 members), (b) medium (5-8 members), and (c) large (more than 8 members). The details are as follows (Table 4.6):

Table 4.6: Family Size of Fish Farmers Surveyed

Districts	*Small (less than 5 members)*	*Medium (5-8 members)*	*Large (more than 8 members)*	*Total*
Lohit	35 (17.50)	97 (48.50)	68 (34.00)	200
Lower Subansiri	12 (12.00)	62 (62.00)	26 (26.00)	100
Total	47 (15.67)	159 (53.00)	94 (31.33)	300

Note: Figures in parentheses indicate the respective percentages of total.
Source: Field Survey, 2010-12.

From Table 4.6, it was found that 15.67 per cent of surveyed fish farmers had small family, 53 per cent had medium family and 31.33 per cent had large family. It was also observed that 34 per cent of surveyed fish farmers in Lohit district had large family size. This may be due to the fact that in Lohit district the size of fish pond was relatively big.

The gender distribution of surveyed fish farmer's household heads is given in the Table 4.7.

Table 4.7: Gender-wise Distribution of Fish Farmers Surveyed

Districts	*Male*	*Female*	*Total*
Lohit	183 (91.50)	17 (8.50)	200
Lower Subansiri	96 (96.00)	4 (4.00)	100
Total	279 (93.00)	21 (7.00)	300

Note: Figures in parentheses indicate the respective percentages of total.
Source: Field Survey, 2010-12.

Table 4.7 shows that most of the surveyed fish farmers (93 per cent) were male. However, it is interesting to observe that around 8.5 per cent of surveyed fish farmers were females in case of Lohit district.

Although the majority of reported fish farmers were males but female household members were actively involved in fish farming activities. Hence, an attempt was made to examine the gender role in fish farming activities in the surveyed districts. For this purpose six major fishing related activities were taken into accounts which are as follows:

1. Preparation of pond;
2. Collection of fingerling (fish seed);
3. Collection of fish feed;
4. Feeding the fish;
5. Harvesting of fish; and
6. Marketing of fish.

It was found that there was a contrasting picture regarding the gender role on the basis of fish farming activities. The marketing activity was purely a male dominated affair in the Lohit district with 97 per cent of marketing activities were done by the males only. On the other hand, in the case of Lower Subansiri district it was found that it is purely a female activity with 100 per cent female participation in the marketing and selling of fish in the market. The preparation of pond is basically a male dominated job with contribution of 59.67 per cent. However, it was observed that in Lohit district males played a more significant role in the preparation of pond (88 per cent). Again it was observed that, in Lower Subansiri pond preparation was jointly done by both male and female (97 per cent). Feeding the fish is also an important activity where women played a more important role in both the districts. Harvesting is an activity in which both males and females were actively participating with 90.67 per cent of total contribution. It was interesting to observe that the joint contribution was found to be 100 per cent in Lower Subansiri district since it is purely a community activity. The details are shown in Table 4.8.

The average working hours for fishing related activity is an

Table 4.8: Gender's Roles in Fish Farming Activities among Surveyed Fish Farmers Household

	Major Activities	*Only Male*	*Both Male and Female*	*Only Female*
Lohit	Preparation of pond	176 (88.00)	24 (8.00)	00
	Collection of fingerling	97 (48.50)	85 (42.50)	18 (9.00)
	Collection of fish feed	87 (43.50)	102 (51.00)	11 (5.50)
	Feeding the fish	21 (10.50)	82 (41.00)	97 (48.50)
	Harvesting of fish	25 (12.50)	172 (86.00)	3 (1.50)
	Marketing of fish	194 (97.00)	4 (2.00)	2 (1.00)
Lower Subansiri	Preparation of pond	3 (3.00)	97 (97.00)	00
	Collection of fingerling	3 (3.00)	48 (48.00)	49 (49.00)
	Collection of fish feed	2 (2.00)	38 (38.00)	60 (60.00)
	Feeding the fish	4 (4.00)	27 (27.00)	69 (69.00)
	Harvesting of fish	00	100 (100.00)	00
	Marketing of fish	00	00	100 (100.00)
Total	Preparation of pond	179 (59.67)	121 (40.33)	00
	Collection of fingerling	100 (33.33)	133 (43.33)	67 (22.24)
	Collection of fish feed	89 (29.67)	140 (46.67)	71 (23.66)
	Feeding the fish	25 (8.33)	109 (36.33)	166 (55.34)
	Harvesting of fish	25 (8.33)	272 (90.67)	3 (1.00)
	Marketing of fish	194 (64.67)	4 (1.33)	102 (34.00)

Note: Figures in parentheses indicate the respective percentages of total.
Source: Field Survey, 2010-12.

important variable and it was found that half (50.33 per cent) of the surveyed fish farmers were engaged in fishing activity for one to two hours daily during the fishing season. However, in the case of Lower Subansiri district, it was found that more than two-sssthird (77 per cent) of surveyed fish farmers were devoting more than two hours in fishing related activity. The details are shown in Table 4.9.

Occupational Structure of Surveyed Fish Farmers

All the fish farmers under the study area were engaged in fish production but none of them had fish farming as the main occupation or primary occupation i.e., occupation which generated

Table 4.9: Average Working Hours by Surveyed Fish Farmers per Day during the Fishing Seasons

Districts	*Less than One Hours*	*One to Two Hours*	*More than Two Hours*	*Total*
Lohit	23 *(11.50)*	133 *(66.50)*	44 *(22.00)*	200
Lower Subansiri	5 *(5.00)*	18 *(18.00)*	77 *(77.00)*	100
Total	28 *(9.33)*	151 *(50.33)*	121 *(40.34)*	300

Note: Figures in parentheses indicate the respective percentages of total.
Source: Field Survey, 2010-12.

either comparatively more employment or more income.

However, in our survey it was found that all of the fish farmers were doing fishing as the second most important occupation or third most important occupation which is considered as secondary occupation or tertiary occupations respectively. All the primary occupations of the respc lents were characterized into seven groups i.e., agriculture, horticulture, animal husbandry, forestry, services, business and others. Agriculture was found to be the major occupation for the respondents (80.33 per cent). In case of Lohit district 77 per cent of the respondents were having agriculture as the primary occupation followed by horticulture (7.5 per cent) and animal husbandry (5 per cent). But in case of Lower Subansiri district only three major types of occupation of respondents were found, i.e., agriculture (87 per cent), services (7 per cent) and business (4 per cent). The details are given in Table 4.10.

Table 4.10: Occupational Structure of Fish Farmers Surveyed

Districts	*Primary Occupations*							
	A	*H*	*AH*	*Fo*	*S*	*B*	*Others*	*Total*
Lohit	154 (77.00)	15 (7.50)	10 (5.00)	5 (2.50)	6 (3.00)	7 (3.50)	3 (1.50)	200
Lower Subansiri	87 (87.00)	0	0	0	7 (7.00)	4 (4.00)	2 (2.00)	100
Total	241 (80.33)	15 (5.00)	10 (3.33)	5 (1.67)	13 (4.33)	11 (3.67)	5 (1.67)	300

Note: Figures in parentheses indicate the respective percentages of total. A: Agriculture, H: Horticulture, AH: Animal Husbandry: Fo: Forestry, S: Service, B: Business, Other: Other occupations than the above mentioned occupations.

Source: Field Survey, 2010-12.

The experience in fishing is also an important variable which influence the production of fish to a great extent. The experience in fish production of the respondents is given in Table 4.11.

Table 4.11: Experience in Fishing Related Activities of Fish Farmers Surveyed

Districts	*0-3 years*	*4-10 years*	*11-20 years*	*More than 20 years*	*Total*
Lohit	9 (4.50)	23 (11.50)	49 (24.50)	119 (59.50)	200
Lower Subansiri	4 (4.00)	8 (8.00)	36 (36.00)	52 (52.00)	100
Total	13 (4.34)	31 (10.33)	85 (28.33)	171 (57.00)	300

Note: Figures in parentheses indicate the respective percentages of total.
Source: Field Survey, 2010-12.

Table 4.11 shows that most of the surveyed fish farmers (57 per cent) had the experience of fish production of more than 20 years. Only 4.34 per cent of surveyed fish farmers were having fish farming experience of less than 3 years. However in case of Lohit district it was found that 59.5 per cent of surveyed fish farmers were experience of fish production of more than 20 years.

Livelihood Linkages of the Fish Farmer Surveyed

A livelihood, according to Frank Ellis, 'comprises the capabilities, assets (including both material and social resources), gender recreations and property rights to support and to sustain a given standard of living. The multiplicity of livelihood sources helps rural households to divert risks and manage uncertainty through allocation of resources. However, in this section, an attempt is made to examine the linkages of fisheries and rural livelihood in the surveyed villages

There are eleven categories of livelihood which were identified in the surveyed villages of Lohit and Lower Subansiri districts. They are as follows:

1. Agriculture and fishery;
2. Agriculture, animal husbandry and fishery;
3. Agriculture, horticulture, animal husbandry and fishery;
4. Agriculture, horticulture and fishery;

5. Agriculture, animal husbandry, forestry and fishery;
6. Agriculture, forestry and fishery;
7. Agriculture, animal husbandry, horticulture, forestry and fishery;
8. Agriculture, services, business and fishery;
9. Agriculture, services and fishery;
10. Agriculture, business and fishery; and
11. Other combinations.

The details are shown in Table 4.12.

Table 4.12: Distribution of Households on the basis of Major Livelihood Strategies in the Surveyed Areas

Livelihood Combinations	*Lohit*	*Lower Subansiri*	*Total*
Agriculture and fishery	65 (32.50)	39 (39.00)	104 (34.67)
Agriculture, animal husbandry and fishery	23 (11.50)	18 (18.00)	41 (13.67)
Agriculture, horticulture, animal husbandry and fishery	36 (18.00)	10 (10.00)	46 (15.33)
Agriculture, horticulture and fishery	15 (7.50)	8 (8.00)	23 (7.67)
Agriculture, animal husbandry, forestry and fishery	14 (7.00)	5 (5.00)	19 (6.33)
Agriculture, forestry and fishery	4 (2.00)	2 (2.00)	6 (2.00)
Agriculture, animal husbandry, horticulture, forestry and fishery	8 (4.00)	4 (4.00)	12 (4.00)
Agriculture, services, business and fishery	14 (7.00)	2 (2.00)	16 (5.33)
Agriculture, services and fishery	4 (2.00)	5 (5.00)	9 (3.00)
Agriculture, business and fishery	6 (3.00)	3 (3.00)	9 (3.00)
Others	11 (5.50)	4 (4.00)	15 (5.00)
Total	200	100	300

Note: Figures in parentheses indicate the respective percentages of total.
Source: Field Survey, 2010-12.

From Table 4.12, it is found that livelihood combination of agriculture and fishery has the highest share (34.67 per cent) with 32.5 per cent in Lohit district and 39 per cent in Lower Subansiri district. It was also observed from the survey that agriculture, horticulture, animal husbandry and fishery was the second largest combination (18 per cent) followed by agriculture, animal husbandry and fishery (11.5 per cent). However, in the case of Lower Subansiri district, the second most important combination is agriculture, animal husbandry and fishery (18 per cent) followed by agriculture, horticulture, animal husbandry and fishery (10 per cent). So from Table 4.12 it is clear that agriculture is the most important source of income for the surveyed fish farmers, and fishery is the additional source of livelihood in the surveyed areas. It is interesting to observe that in most of the surveyed households in Lower Subansiri district, paddy-cum-fish culture was popular. It is a role model for other districts of Arunachal Pradesh. However, in Lohit district, in some of the surveyed villages, fish-cum-duck culture was found to be conducted successfully.

Finally, an attempt was made to examine the share of income from different sources under various livelihood combinations in the surveyed districts. The details are given in Table 4.13

Table 4.13: Distribution of Share of Income from Different Sources under various Livelihood Combinations in the Surveyed Districts

Livelihood Combinations	*Share in per cent*						
	A	*F*	*H*	*AH*	*Fo*	*S*	*B*
Agriculture and fishery	72.26	27.74	—	—	—	—	—
Agriculture, animal husbandry and fishery	49.29	25.38	—	25.33	—	—	—
Agriculture, horticulture, animal husbandry and fishery	40.02	31.46	10.39	18.13	—	—	—
Agriculture, horticulture and fishery	67.25	22.25	10.50	—	—	—	—
Agriculture, animal husbandry, forestry and fishery	40.33	10.33	—	29.31	20.03	—	—
Agriculture , forestry and fishery	65.00	18.29	—	—	16.71	—	—
Agriculture, animal husbandry, horticulture, forestry and fishery	44.29	20.13	—	20.00	15.58	—	—
Agriculture, services, business and fishery	24.12	19.00	—	—	—	24.36	32.52
Agriculture, services and fishery	22.59	7.16	—	—	—	70.25	—
Agriculture, business and fishery	29.59	26.40	—	—	—	—	44.01

Note: A : Agriculture, F: Fishery, H: Horticulture, AH: Animal Husbandry, Fo : Forestry, S: Services and B: Business.

Source: Field Survey, 2010-12.

From Table 4.13 it was found that the share of income from fishery varied from 7.16 per cent (agriculture, services and fishery combination) to 31.46 per cent (agriculture, horticulture, animal husbandry and fishery combination). It was also observed that the combination of fishery to total income was relatively more when it was combined with animal husbandry along with other combinations. It was relatively less when it was combined with services along with other combinations. This may be due to the fact that fish rearing and animal husbandry are related activity Secondly, fish rearing a time consuming activity which may be difficult to combine along with services.

Operational Features of the Sampled P onds

On the basis of ownership of ponds it was found that most of the sampled ponds (65.36 per cent) were found to be operated by single pond owners. Relatively a small proportion of water units were owned by two or more than two owners in the study area. The details are given in Figure 4.1.

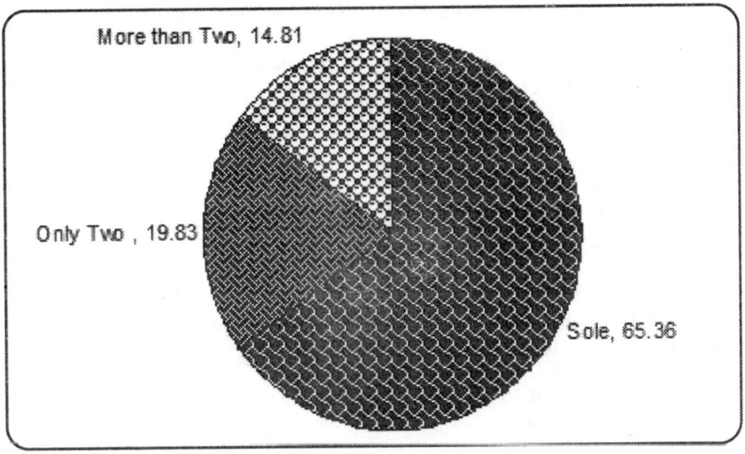

Source: Field Survey, 2010-12.

Fig. 4.1: Distribution of Ownership of Ponds *(in per cent)*

The sampled water units were also used for other purposes, i.e., other than fish production, like irrigation purpose, duck rearing, cattle watering, pig rearing, household purposes, etc.

Majority of the sampled water units were used for multipurpose activities. It was found that a major proportion of the water units were used for irrigation purposes (59.38 per cent) followed by household purpose (27.25 per cent) and then for watering and rearing of birds and animals (21.23 per cent). The details are provided in Figure 4.2.

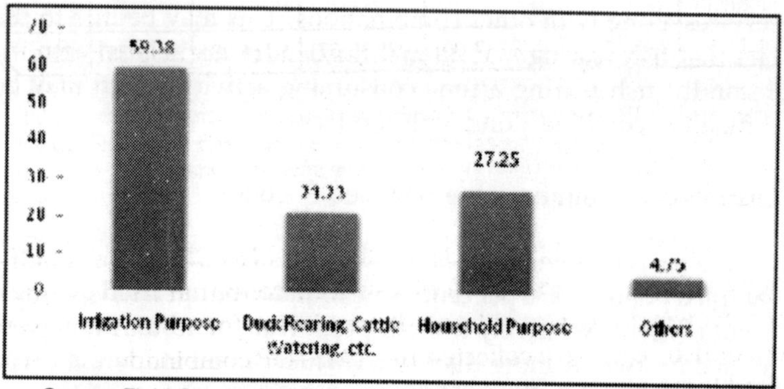

Source: Field Survey, 2010-12.

Fig. 4.2: Use of Water Units Other than Fishery Activities *(in per cent)*

There are four major sources of fish seed collection identified in the area of our study:

1. Government Supply (GS),
2. Market Source (MS),
3. Own Pond (OP), and
4. Other Source.

On the basis of the above mentioned four sources, five major combinations were structured from where major portion of fish seed were collected by fish farmers in the area of our study.

1. Government Supply (GS) + Market Source (MS) + Own Pond (OP);
2. Government Supply (GS) + Market Source (MS);
3. Market Source (MS) + Own Pond (OP);
4. Government Supply (GS) + Own Pond (OP);
5. Other combinations.

The details are given in the Table 4.14.

Table 4.14: Combinations of Major Source of Collection of Fish Seeds

Districts	*GS+MS+OP*	*GS+MS*	*MS+OP*	*GS+OP*	*Other*	*Total*
Lohit	74 (37.00)	12 (6.00)	95 (47.50)	10 (5.00)	9 (4.50)	200
Lower Subansiri	69 (69.00)	9 (9.00)	12 (12.00)	3 (3.00)	7 (7.00)	100
Total	143 (47.67)	21 (7.00)	107 (35.67)	13 (4.33)	16 (5.33)	300

Note : Figures in parentheses indicate the respective percentages of total. Government Source: GS, Market Source: MS, Own Pond: OP, Other: Other combination than the above mentioned combinations.

Source: Field Survey, 2010-12.

From Table 4.14 it is clear that GS+MS+OP is the major combination (47.67 per cent) of fish seed collection in the study area. However, in case of Lohit district it was found that 47.5 per cent of fish seed were collected from MS+OP combination. It was found that a major portion of fish seed were either used from own pond or collected from private hatchery.

Ponds and water bodies vary in size and, therefore, a study of the size of sampled water units would be relevant for economic analysis. The ponds and water bodies were grouped into three different size classes like small (up to 0.29 acres), medium (0.30 to 1.99 acres) and large (2.00 acres and above). The details are given in Table 4.15.

Table 4.15: Size Class Distribution of the Numbers and Area of Currently Operated Water Units

Districts	*Small (Up to 0.29 acres)*	*Medium (0.30 to 1.99 acres)*	*Large (2.00 acres and above)*	*Total*
Lohit	89 (35.18)	100 (39.53)	64 (25.29)	253
Lower Subansiri	97 (92.38)	8 (7.62)	00	105
Total	186 (51.96)	108 (30.17)	64 (17.87)	358

Note: Figures in parentheses indicate the respective percentages of total.

Source: Field Survey, 2010-12.

From Table 4.15 it is found that the size of ponds and water bodies vary significantly in the plains and hilly districts. For example, in the surveyed plain district of Lohit, most of the ponds (64.52 per cent) consisted of medium and large size. On the other hand, in the surveyed hilly district like Lower Subansiri, most of the ponds (92.38 per cent) consisted of small category only.

References

Choudhary *et al.* (2008): *Indigenous Knowledge and Policy Issues in Fisheries,* National Bureau of Fish Genetic Resources, ICAR, Lucknow.

Ellis, F. (1993): *Peasant Economics: Farm Households and Agrarian Development*, 2nd ed., Cambridge University Press, Great Britain.

Government of Arunachal Pradesh (2006): *Arunachal Pradesh District Gazetteers: Lohit District,* Directorate of Information and Public Relation, Itanagar.

Government of Arunachal Pradesh (2008): *Arunachal Pradesh District Gazetteers: Subansiri District,* Directorate of Information and Public Relation, Itanagar.

Government of Arunachal Pradesh (2011): *Statistical Abstract of Arunachal Pradesh,* Directorate of Economics and Statistics, Itanagar.

Government of India (2009): *Arunachal Pradesh Development Report,* Planning Commission, New Delhi.

Government of India (2011): *Provisional Population Totals: Paper 2, Vol. 1 of 2011 Rural-Urban Distribution of Arunachal Pradesh Series 13,* Census of India 2011.

Inoni, O.E. (2007): "Allocative Efficiency in Pond Fish Production in Delta State, Nigeria: A Production Function Approach", *Agricultura Tropica ET Subtropica,* Vol. 40, No. 4, pp. 127-134.

Chapter - 5

Productivity, Resource Use Efficiency and Marketing Structure

A Quantitative Analysis

Introduction

Fish production is dependent on various factors such as pond preparation, control of weeds, liming, proper stocking, monitoring of physical-chemical parameters, use of manures, supplementary feeding, netting, stock manipulation, harvesting, etc. It is sometimes observed that suboptimal input use has led to a high cost of fish production and resulted in low returns. Few serious attempts have been made to identify the key input factors and their contribution to fish production. Hence, there is a need for developing an optimal resource management strategy and the appraisal of resource management strategy. With this background, in this chapter an attempt was made to analyse the productivity, factors of variations in productivity, resource–use efficiency, gross margin and net margin; profitability estimates as well as marketing structure of the study area.

Productivity Analysis of Surveyed Fish Ponds

In this section, an attempt is made to estimate the productivity of fish pond on different size classes. Firstly, the surveyed ponds were divided into three different size classes, i.e., small (up to 0.29 acres), medium (0.30 to 1.99 acres) and large (2.00 acres and above). Then the productivity was measured in terms of kg of fish catch per acre per year in the three different categories of ponds.

The productivity of small size pond was found to be 506.14 kg/acre/year followed by medium size (422.13 kg/acre/year) and large size (304.54 kg/acre/year). Thus, it was observed that there was inverse relationship between the size of pond and productivity. The inverse relationship was found to be more specific in the case of Lohit district where the productivity of the small size pond was found to be 509.30 kg/acre/year whereas, the productivity of medium size pond was 416.69 kg/acre/year and that of large size pond was 304.54 kg/acre/year. On the other hand, the inverse relationship was not very specific in the case of hilly districts of Lower Subansiri where the productivity of small size pond was found to be 503.24 kg/acre/year and that of medium size pond was 490.16 kg/acre/year. The large size pond was not found in the surveyed area of Lower Subansiri district. The productivity of small size pond was much higher than that of the medium and large size pond because of the fact that the water bodies of smaller size enjoy the benefits of close supervision, intimate monitoring and sincere regulation by the family members themselves. The details are given in Table 5.1 below:

Table 5.1: Distribution of Productivity by Size of Pond

(in kg/acre/year)

Pond Size	*Lohit*	*Lower Subansiri*	*Aggregate Productivity*
Small	509.30	503.24	506.14
Medium	416.69	490.16	422.13
Large	304.54	—	304.54
All	420.00	502.24	444.76

Source: Field Survey, 2010-2012.

It was observed that between the two surveyed districts, on an average the productivity of fish in Lohit district (420 kg/acre/year) was found to be much lower than that of Lower Subansiri district (502.24 kg/acre/year). However, in the case of small size ponds, the productivity of fish in Lohit district was marginally higher than that of Lower Subansiri district.

Another important observation of the surveyed pond was that there was a decline in productivity of pond as the number of shareholders increased. The productivity of sole owner pond was found to be 496.02 kg/acre/year, followed by two owners (364.97 kg/acre/year) and more than two owners (311.64 kg/acre/year).

From Table 5.2 it is found that in the case of Lohit district the productivity of one owner, two owners and more than two owners pond were found to be as high as 496.32 kg/acre/year, 308.52 kg/acre/year and 254.39 kg/acre/year respectively. But it was interesting to observe that the trend is 'U'-shaped in the case of Lower Subansiri district where productivity of one owner, two owners and more than two owner ponds were found to be 502.24 kg/acre/year, 499.36 kg/acre/year and 507.26 kg/acre/year respectively. It showed that as the number of owners increased the productivity first declined in Lower Subansiri district and then it increased. However, there was a variation in the relationship of productivity and number of pond owner in the case of the surveyed districts. The details are given in Table. 5.2

Table 5.2: Distribution of Productivity by Number of Owners of Pond

(in kg/acre/ year)

Number of Owner	*Lohit*	*Lower Subansiri*	*Aggregate Productivity*
One	496.32	502.24	496.02
Two	308.52	499.36	364.97
More than Two	254.39	507.26	311.64
All	420.00	502.24	444.76

Source: Field Survey, 2010-2012.

This variation in the two districts may be due to two factors. Firstly, Lower Subansiri is basically a hilly district and Lohit is a comparatively plain district and both the districts are from two different agro climatic zones of the State. Secondly, in Lower Subansiri district, paddy-cum-fish culture is practiced on a very large scale.

Now, it is important to analyse the relationship between the productivity of fish pond with different variables like socio-economic characteristics, cost of production, infrastructural facilities, etc., separately for these two districts. So, separate regression models were used for these two districts to get a clear result.

Results and Interpretation of Regression Analysis

For Lohit district, the following regression model was used to analyse the effect of different variables (X_i) like socio-economic characteristics, cost of production, infrastructural facilities, etc., on the productivity of fish (Y) in the sampled ponds. The regression equation is given below:

$$\ln Y = \alpha + \beta_1 X_1 + \beta_2 X_2 + \beta_3 X_3 + \beta_4 X_4 + \beta_5 X_5 + \beta_6 X_6 + \beta_7 X_7 + \beta_8 X_8 + \beta_9 X_9 + \beta_{10} X_{10} + \beta_{11} X_{11} + \beta_{12} X_{12} + \beta_{13} X_{13} + \beta_{14} X_{14} + U_t \rightarrow 5.1$$

Where,

Y = Productivity of fish *(kg/acre);*

X_1 = Age of the fish farmers *(in years);*

X_2 = Gender of fish farmers *(dummy variable, female = 0 and male = 1);*

X_3 = Educational level *(in years);*

X_4 = Family size;

X_5 = Pond size *(in acres);*

X_6 = Fish seed (fingerlings) *(in 50 Nos/acre);*

X_7 = Fish Feed *(in kg/acre);*

X_8 = Manure, Fertilizer, lime etc. *(in kg/acre);*

X_9 = Experience in fishery related activities *(in years);*

X_{10} = Distance of water bodies *(in 10 metres);*

X_{11} = Total working hours (hired + family labour) *(man day/acre);*

X_{12} = Training received *(dummy variable, No=0 and Yes = 1);*

X_{13} = Distance from market area *(in kms);*

X_{14} = Number of pond owners;

α = Constant;

β_i = Coefficient of the ith variable (i = 1-14); and

U_t = Error term *(assumed to have a zero mean and constant variance)*

The regression result is presented in the equation below:

$$\ln Y = 2.494 \underset{(-0.497)}{- 0.007X_1} \underset{(0.053)}{+ 0.008X_2} \underset{(-0.185)}{- 0.021X_3}$$

$$+0.074^{***}X_4 \underset{(1.052)}{} \quad -0.139^{*}X_5 \underset{(-3.092)}{} \quad +2.810^{*}X_6 \underset{(2.019)}{} \quad +1.200^{***}X_7 \underset{(1.166)}{}$$

$$+1.340X_8 \underset{(0.053)}{} \quad +0.045^{**}X_9 \underset{(1.344)}{} \quad -3.165^{**}X_{10} \underset{(-1.526)}{} \quad +0.150X_{11} \underset{(0.244)}{}$$

$$+0.007^{**}X_{12} \underset{(1.890)}{} \quad -2.951^{***}X_{13} \underset{(-1.153)}{} \quad -0.255^{*}X_{14} \underset{(-2.397)}{} \qquad \rightarrow 5.2$$

$R^2 = 0.751, \bar{R}^2 = 0.676, F = 9.991^*$ and $N = 200$

Note: 1. Figures in the parentheses indicate the respective t-values of the estimated coefficients.

2. *, ** and *** denote that the coefficient are significant at 1%, 5% and 10% level of probability respectively.

Source: Field Survey, 2010-2012.

The R^2 for the estimated regression showed that about 75.1 per cent of variation in the productivity of fish pond in the study area was explained by the explanatory variables (X_i) and the remaining 24.9 per cent was unexplained due to random variable (U_t).

It was evident from the analysis that eight of the estimators of the explanatory variables, i.e., gender (X_2), family size (X_4), fish seed (X_6), fish feed (X_7), manures, fertilizer, lime etc. (X_8); experience in fishery related activity (X_9), total working hours (X_{11}) and training received (X_{12}) have a positive sign which indicates that any increase of the eight variables would increase the productivity of fish pond. Among these eight variables five were significant at different levels. The explanatory variable like fish seed was found to be statistically significant at 0.01 levels. The variables such as experience in fishery related activity and training received were found to be statistically significant at 0.05 levels. The other variables like fish feed and family size were significant at 0.10 levels. The rest of the variables like gender, manure, fertilizer, lime, etc, and total working hour had positive coefficient but were not significant. Among fourteen explanatory variables, six variables like age (X_1), education level (X_3), pond size (X_5), distance of water bodies (X_{10}), distance from market (X_{13}) and number of pond owners (X_{14}) were found to be negatively related.

It is interesting to observe that age and education were found to be negatively related but they were not significant. The variables like number of pond owners and pond size had not only negative coefficient but they were significant at 0.01 level. This means that the higher number of pond owners and the larger the pond size, the lower was the productivity from the surveyed ponds. The other variables like distance of water bodies and distance from market were not only negative but were significant at 0.05 and 0.10 levels respectively

Since, in the case of Lower Subansiri, district paddy-cum-fish culture is practised on a very large scale, an additional variable, i.e., cultivable land area is included in the regression equation of 5.1. The new regression equation is given as:

$$\ln Y = \alpha + \beta_1 X_1 + \beta_2 X_2 + \beta_3 X_3 + \beta_4 X_4 + \beta_5 X_5 + \beta_6 X_6 + \beta_7 X_7 + \beta_8 X_8 + \beta_9 X_9 + \beta_{10} X_{10} + \beta_{11} X_{11} + \beta_{12} X_{12} + \beta_{13} X_{13} + \beta_{14} X_{14} + \beta_{15} X_{15} + U_t \rightarrow 5.3$$

Where,

Y = Productivity of fish *(kg/acre);*

X_1 = Age of the fish farmers *(in years);*

X_2 = Gender of fish farmers *(dummy variable, female = 0 and male = 1);*

X_3 = Educational level *(in years);*

X_4 = Family size;

X_5 = Pond size *(in acres);*

X_6 = Fish seed (fingerlings) *(in 50Nos. /acre);*

X_7 = Fish Feed *(in kg/acre);*

X_8 = Manure, Fertilizer, lime etc. *(in kg/acre);*

X_9 = Experience in fishery related activities *(in years);*

X_{10} = Distance of water bodies *(in 10 metres);*

X_{11} = Total working hours (hired + family labour) *(man day/acre);*

X_{12} = Training received *(dummy variable, No=0 and Yes = 1);*

X_{13} = Distance from market area *(in km);*

X_{14} = Number of pond owners;

X_{15} = Cultivable land area *(in hectares);*

α = Constant;

β_i = Coefficient of the ith variable (i = 1-15); and

U_t= Error term *(assumed to have a zero mean and constant variance)*

The regression result is presented in the equation 5.4 below:

$$
\begin{array}{lllll}
\ln Y = 2.238 & + 0.002X_1 & + 0.045X_2 & + 0.201^{***}X_3 & \\
 & (0.129) & (0.095) & (1.841) & \\
+ 0.139^{*}X_4 & - 0.010^{***}X_5 & + 2.739^{***} & + 2.810^{**}X_7 & \\
(4.032) & (-1.432) & X_6(1.142) & (2.903) & \\
+ 2.190X_8 & + 0.138^{*}X_9 & + 0.001X_{10} & + 1.990^{**}X_{11} & \\
(0.009) & (4.092) & (0.053) & (2.297) & \\
+ 0.015X_{12} & - 1.450^{*}X_{13} & - 0.067X_{14} & + 0.058X_{15} & \\
(0.209) & (-3.420) & (-0.576) & (0.874) & \rightarrow 5.4
\end{array}
$$

R^2= 0.733, $\bar{R}^2$ = 0.653, F = 9.099* and N = 100

Note: 1. Figures in the parentheses indicate the respective t-values of the estimated coefficients.

2. *, ** and *** denote that the coefficient are significant at 1%, 5% and 10% level of probability respectively.

3. As paddy-cum-fish culture is practiced on a very large scale in Lower Subansiri district, therefore, the input used in the production were divided as per the proportion of value of outputs, i.e., paddy and fish.

Source: Field Survey, 2010-2012.

The R^2 for the estimated regression was found to be 73.3 per cent, which indicate the amount variation was explained by the explanatory variables and remaining 26.7 per cent was unexplained. It was found from the analysis that twelve explanatory variables like age of the fish farmers (X_1), gender (X_2), education level (X_3), family size (X_4), fish seed (X_5), pond size (X_6), fish feed (X_7), manure, fertilizer, lime etc. (X_8), experience in fishing related activity (X_9), distance of water bodies (X_{10}), total working hours (X_{11}), training received (X_{12}) and cultivable land area (X_{15}) had positive signs which indicates that any increase in any of these variable would increase the productivity of fish ponds. Among these twelve explanatory variables six were significant at different level of probability. For example, explanatory variables like experience in fishery related activity and family size were found to be significant at 0.01 levels. The explanatory variables like fish feed and total working hours were found to be significant at 0.05 levels. The explanatory variables such as fish seed and educational level were found to be significant at 0.10 levels. The rest of the variables like manure, fertilizer, lime, etc., cultivable land area, gender of fish farmer, training received, age of fish farmers and distance of water bodies had positive coefficients but were found to be insignificant.

The remaining three explanatory variables like pond size (X_5), distance from market (X_{13}) and number of pond owners (X_{14}) were found to be negative. However, out of these three explanatory variables, distances from market and pond size were found to be significant at 0.01 and 0.10 level respectively.

Cost Benefit Analysis

Only physical parameters of input and output of fish production may not bring out managerial efficiency. Hence, given the physical quantities of inputs, an attempt was made to compute the average cost of production of fish. At the same time gross margin analysis and profitability ratio were used to examine the cost and benefit of fish farming in the study area.

Gross Margin and Net Return Analysis

Gross margin and net return analysis is given by the equation 5.5 and 5.6 below:

Net Return (**NR**) = Total Revenue (**TR**) – Total Cost (**TC**) → 5.5

Gross Margin (**GM**) = Total Revenue (**TR**) – Variable Cost (**VC**) → 5.6

Table 5.3 shows that as a whole, the total cost of fish was found to be ₹50.69/kg. However, there was large variation of total cost in the different size of pond ranging from ₹57.14/kg in large pond farming to ₹44.12/kg in medium pond farming. However, out of the total cost, 71.36 per cent consisted of variable cost and the rest 28.64 per cent consisted of fixed cost. However, the fixed cost was found to be the highest among small pond owners and variable cost was found to be highest in case of larger pond owners. This may be due to the fact that large pond owners may have to use more hired labour. The total revenue of fish obtained was found to be ₹82.39/kg ranging from ₹85.21/kg in small pond owner to

Table 5.3 : Distribution of Cost and Return Analysis for Fish Production in the Study Area

	Small	Medium	Large	All
Variable Cost (VC) (in ₹/kg)	36.46 (69.74)	31.95 (72.42)	42.46 (74.31)	36.17 (71.36)
Fixed Cost (FC) (in ₹/kg)	15.82 (30.26)	12.17 (27.58)	14.68 (25.69)	14.52 (28.64)
Total Cost (TC) (in ₹/kg)	52.28	44.12	57.14	50.69
Total Revenue (TR) (in ₹/kg)	85.21	80.74	80.00	82.93
Net Return (NR) (in ₹/kg)	32.93	36.62	22.86	32.24
Gross Margin (GM) (in ₹/kg)	48.75	48.79	37.54	46.76

Note: Figures in parentheses indicate the respective percentages of Total Cost (TC).
Source: Field Survey, 2010-12.

₹80.00/kg in large fish farming. This gives the gross margin of ₹46.76/ kg which was high in case of medium fish farming and small fish farming with ₹48.79/kg and ₹48.75/kg respectively. It is interesting to observe that the value of gross margin was significantly low in the case of large fish farming (₹37.54/kg). On the other hand, in the case of net return, the farmers from medium fish farming were found to be the most efficient (₹36.62/kg) as compared to small (₹32.93/kg) and large (₹22.86/kg) pond owners. This is because in case of small pond owners, the fixed cost was relatively high and in case of large pond owners, the variable cost was relatively high. Hence, the analysis shows that there was significant difference in net returns in different size of fish farming.

Profitability Estimates

The performance and economic worth of the fish farmer was determined with the help of the following profitability ratios given in equations 5.7, 5.8 and 5.9 below:

$$\text{Benefit Cost Ratio (BCR)} = \frac{\text{Total Revenue (TR)}}{\text{Total Cost (TC)}} \rightarrow 5.7$$

$$\text{Expense Structure Ratio (ESR)} = \frac{\text{Fixed Cost (FC)}}{\text{Variable Cost (VC)}} \rightarrow 5.8$$

$$\text{Rate of Return (RoR)} = \frac{\text{Net Return (NR)}}{\text{Total Cost (TC)}} \qquad \rightarrow 5.9$$

The Benefit Cost Ratio (BCR) or profitability index is one of the concepts of discount method of operation evaluation. As a rule of thumb, operation with benefit cost greater than one, equal to one or less than one indicates profit, break-even or loss respectively (F.I. Olagunju, *et. al.*, 2007). On this basis, in the study area, the ratio was found to be greater than one, i.e., 1.64 and it indicates that the fish farming is profitable in the study area. However, in order to acquire higher benefit-cost ratio, it is necessary to increase the quality of seed, feed and skilled labour. The benefit-cost ratio values were estimated to be 1.63, 1.83 and 1.4 for small, medium and large pond farmers respectively. The value shows that medium pond farmers were recovering ₹ 1.83 by investing one rupee whereas, small and large pond farmers were recovering ₹1.63 and ₹1.40 respectively. Expense Structure Ratio (ESR) was 0.40 which implies that about 40 per cent of the total cost of production consisted of fixed cost of production. This makes the fish farming worthwhile since an increase in production with variable cost will increase the total revenue leaving the fixed cost unchanged. The expense structure ratio was higher in the case of small pond farming (0.43) followed by medium and large sized pond with 0.38 and 0.35 respectively. The Rate of Return (RoR) in the study area was 0.64 which shows that for every one rupee invested 64 paise was gained by the fish farmer. The details are shown in Table 5.4.

Table 5.4: Distribution of Profitability Estimates for Fish Production in the Study Area

Profitability Estimates	*Small*	*Medium*	*Large*	*All*
Benefit Cost Ratio (BCR)	1.63	1.83	1.40	1.64
Expense Structure Ratio (ESR)	0.43	0.38	0.35	0.40
Rate of Return (RoR)	0.63	0.83	0.40	0.64

Source: Field Survey, 2010-12.

All the estimates showed that there is enough profitability for fish production in the study area irrespective of pond size.

Resource Use Efficiency

The production of fish depends on various factors. Hence, it is necessary to identify the key input factors and their contribution to fish production in the study area. Thus, with the help of production function analysis an attempt was made to establish a relationship between production of fish and different inputs like fish seeds, fertilizers, supplementary fees, manures, labour, etc. The Cobb-Douglas production function was used for the estimation of elasticities of production and returns to scale. The Cobb-Douglas production function is given in equation 5.10:

$$Y = \alpha X_i^{\beta i} u_t \qquad \rightarrow 5.10$$

$$\text{or, } Y = \alpha X_1^{\beta 1} X_2^{\beta 2} X_3^{\beta 3} X_4^{\beta 4} e^u$$

Where,

Y = Value of gross fish production (in ₹);
α = Intercept *(constant);*
X_1 = Fish seed *(₹/50 nos.);*
X_2 = Fish feed *(₹/kg);*
X_3 = Manure, fertilizers, lime, etc *(₹/kg);*
X_4 = Labour cost *(₹/acre);*
u_t = Error term*(assumed to have a zero mean and constant variance);* and
β_1 to β_4 = Regression coefficient or production elasticities of respective variables

The analysis is based on the cross-sectional pond-wise per acre values of output and the values of all the four independent variables as explained above. The Marginal Value Product (MVP) of a variable is given by equation 5.11:

$$MVPx_i = \frac{\partial Y}{\partial Xi} \qquad \rightarrow 5.11$$

$$= \beta i \, \frac{\overline{Y}}{\overline{Xi}}$$

where;

Y = Value of gross fish production;
$\overline{Y}$ = Geometric mean of the value of gross fish production;
X_i = *i*th input;

$\overline{Xi}$ = Geometric mean of the ith input; and

βi = Elasticity of production of the ith input/ Regression coefficient of ith input.

With the help of the above mentioned production function an attempt was also made to estimate production elasticities and marginal value product of two surveyed districts separately. The details are given in Table 5.5.

Table 5.5: Production Elasticities and Marginal Value Products of Various Inputs

Input Variables	*Lohit*		*Lower Subansiri*	
	Production Elasticities	*MVPs (in ₹)*	*Production Elasticities*	*MVPs (in ₹)*
Fish Seeds (X_1)	0.63**(3.601)	2.31	0.54**(4.516)	2.45
Fish Feeds (X_2)	0.52***(2.132)	1.95	0.69**(4.069)	2.56
Manure, fertilizers, lime, etc. (X_3)	0.23 (0.250)	1.66	0.46***(2.304)	1.17
Labour (X_4)	0.39***(2.018)	1.63	0.19(0.557)	1.69
	R^2 = 0.689, $\overline{R}^2$ = 0.684, N = 200 & F = 12.352*		R^2 = 0.664, $\overline{R}^2$ = 0.661, N = 100 & F = 10.326*	

Note: 1. Figures in Parentheses indicates the *t*-value of respective coefficients.
2. *, ** and *** denote that the coefficient are significant at 1%, 5% and 10% level of probability respectively.

Source: Field Survey, 2010-2012.

It is clear from Table 5.5 that the independent variable included in the study affect fish production significantly. In case of Lohit district the estimated value of R^2 is 0.689 which indicates that 68.9 per cent of total variation of fish production (Y) was explained by the four variables i.e., fish seeds (X_1), fish feeds (X_2), manure, fertilizers, lime, etc. (X_3) and labour (X_4). The sum of production of elasticities of all variables under the study was 1.77, which indicates that the increasing returns to scale existed in the production of the sampled ponds. On the other hand, in case of Lower Subansiri the value of R^2 is 0.664 which indicates that the variables explained 66.4 per cent of total variation in the fish production in the sampled ponds. There is also an increasing return to scale (1.88) which is higher than that of Lohit district. This indicates that in case of Lohit district the increase in one per cent of the variables will result in 1.77 per cent increase in fish production and in Lower Subansiri district it will result in 1.88 per cent increase in production. It is also clear from the analysis that the individual production elasticities of fish seeds, fish feeds, manure, fertilizers, lime, etc., and labour are not only positive but also most of the variables are significant. However, a distinct pattern was observed in our sampled districts. For example, in case of Lohit district, the highest expected increase in fish production was observed due to increase in fish seeds (fingerlings) since the coefficient of fish seed was found to be 0.63 which was significant at 0.05 level. Hence, it can be said that in Lohit district an increase in investment in fish seed may help fish farmers to increase the fish production. However, in Lower Subansiri the most important factor of production was found to be fish feed with 0.69 production elasticity values which was significant at 0.05 level. Hence, it can be concluded that in Lower Subansiri district an increase in fish feed will help to increase fish production.

Table 5.5 also shows that Marginal Value Productivities (MVPs) of all the inputs in both the districts were found to be positive. In fact, in all the cases, the values of MVPs were more than one. This explains that an investment of rupee one on any input under our study is likely to increase fish production by more than the value of rupee one. Specifically, in Lohit district an investment of one rupee in fish seed was likely to generate an additional income to the extent of ₹2.31. On the other hand, in Lower Subansiri rupee one investment in fish feed was likely to generate an additional income to the extent of ₹2.56. Of course, it largely depends also upon the price of fish. All these estimates and analysis of resource-use efficiency, gross margin and net return and profitability estimates suggest that there exists ample scope for improvement of fish production through appropriate input allocation.

Marketing Structure in the Surveyed Districts

Marketing is one of the most important aspects in fish production as it is a highly perishable commodity. The marketing activity is restricted mainly to nearby markets like Tezu, Namsai, Mahadevpur and Sunpura in Lohit district and Hapoli in Lower Subansiri district. So, an attempt was also made to analyse the different marketing aspects like identification of important channels, cost and margins involved in fish marketing in the surveyed area. It was found that there are basically three channels through which fish is marketed in the surveyed area.

Channel-I: Producer → Retailer → Consumer

Channel-II: Producer → Vendor → Consumer

Channel-III: Producer → Consumer

Table 5.6: Disposal of Fish through Different Marketing Channels

	Channel I	*Channel II*	*Channel III*	*Total*
Lohit	137 (68.50)	33 (16.50)	30 (15.00)	200
Lower Subansiri	61 (61.00)	00	39 (39.00)	100
Total	198 (66.00)	33 (11.00)	69 (23.00)	300

Note: Figures in parentheses indicate the respective percentages of total.
Source: Field Survey, 2010-12.

From Table 5.6 it is observed that channel I (66 per cent) was the most popular channel followed by channel III (23 per cent) and channel II (11 per cent) respectively. The channel II existed only in one district, i.e., In Lohit district among the two surveyed districts but it was the second important channel with 16.5 per cent share.

It was also observed from Table 5.7 that the producers share in consumer's rupee varied from 64.29 per cent to 72.73 per cent in the marketing of fish through identified channels. The details are provided in Table 5.7.

From Table 5.7 it was found that the marketing margin was quite high particularly in channel I. A comparatively lower

Table 5.7: Marketing Cost, Margin and Prices in the Study Area

(in ₹/kg)

Districts	*Particulars*	*Channel-I*	*Channel-II*
Lohit	Producer's Price	80.00 (66.68)	80.00 (72.73)
	Marketing Cost	12.45 (10.36)	9.38 (8.53)
	Marketing Margin	27.55 (22.96)	20.62 (18.74)
	Price paid by Consumer	120.00 (100.00)	110.00 (100.00)
Lower Subansiri	Producer's Price	90.00 (64.29)	—
	Marketing Cost	17.25 (12.32)	—
	Marketing Margin	32.75 (23.39)	—
	Price paid by Consumer	140.00 (100.00)	—

Note: Figures in parentheses indicate the respective percentages of total, i.e., price paid by the consumer.

Source: Field Survey, 2010-12.

producer's share in consumer's rupee in channel I and channel II was mainly because of the presence of agents who corner their margins by providing services in the fish marketing. Thus, though these two parameters, namely producer's share in consumer's rupee as well as quantum of costs and margins indicate that existing system of fish marketing in the study area was by and large inefficient. In fact, it was found that marketing system was quite unorganized to a great disadvantage to the fish pond owners.

Marketing Efficiency in the Study Area

In order to know the degree of the market performance, it is important to know the marketing efficiency. The efficiency of various identified marketing channels in the study area was calculated through the Shepherd's formula. The formula is given by equation 5.12:

$$ME = \frac{V}{I} - I \qquad \rightarrow 5.12$$

where;

ME = Index of marketing efficiency;

V = Value of goods sold (consumer's price); and

I = Total marketing cost.

Table 5.8: Estimates of Marketing Efficiency in Different Marketing Channels

Districts	*Particulars*	*Channel-I*	*Channel-II*
Lohit	Consumer's Price *(in ₹/kg)*	120	110
	Marketing Cost *(in ₹/kg)*	12.45	9.36
	Marketing Efficiency	8.64	10.75
Lower Subansiri	Consumer's Price *(in ₹/kg)*	140	—
	Marketing Cost *(in ₹/kg)*	17.25	—
	Marketing Efficiency	7.12	—

Source: Field Survey, 2010-12.

Table 5.8 represents that the estimates of marketing efficiency of fish through various channels through Shepherd's formula. It shows that the marketing efficiency is higher in channel-II in Lohit district (10.75) and lowest in the channel-I of Lower Subansiri district (7.12).

From the above analysis of the chapter it was found that there was an inverse relationship between pond size and productivity. However, there were wide variations in the relationship of productivity and pond size in case of surveyed districts. This may be due to the fact that two districts are located in two different agro climatic zones. Further, in Lower Subansiri district paddy-cum-fish culture is practised on a very large scale. However, it is interesting to observe that in both the districts increasing returns to scale existed. The analysis further showed that the marginal value productivities of all the inputs are found to be positive and in all the cases, the marginal value productivities have values more than one. This shows that there is ample scope for improvement of fish production through appropriate input allocation. However, the parameters like producer's share in consumer's rupee as well as quantum of costs and margin indicate that existing system of fish marketing in the study area was by and large inefficient.

References

Chakraborty, G. (2007): *An Economic Analysis of the Development of the Char Areas of Assam with Special Reference to Barpeta District*, (Ph.D.

Thesis submitted to the Department of Economics, Dibrugarh University, Assam).

Misra J. (2009): *Problems and Prospects of Inland Aquaculture in West Bengal – A Case Study*, (Ph.D. Thesis).

Misra, S. R. (2006): *Inland Fisheries in India: Issues and Concerns*, Concept Publishing Company, New Delhi.

Misra, S. R. (2012): *Sustainable Rural Livelihood Systems: The Case for India's Inland Fisheries Sector*, Concept Publishing Company (P) Ltd., New Delhi.

Olagunju, F. I. *et al.* (2007): "Economic Viability of Cat Fish Production in Oyo State, Nigeria", *Journal of Human Ecology*, Vol. 21, No. 2, pp. 121-124.

Olubunmi, A.and A. F. Bankole (2012): "Determinants of Income from Fish Marketing in Ibarapa Area of Oyo State, Nigeria", *Science Journal of Agricultural Research and Management*, Vol. 2012, Article ID sjarm-135, 6 pp.

Patil, A. (2012): "Economic Valuation of Reservoirs in Terms of Agricultural Productivity and Fishery in Dry Region of Sangli District, Maharashtra", *Biological Forum—An International Journal*, Vol. 4, No. 21, pp. 10-14.

Sheperd, G.S. (1965). Farm Products-Economic Analysis. Iowa State University Press, Iowa, USA.

Chapter - 6

Constraints for Adoption of Fish Farming and Evaluation of Government Policies regarding Fisheries

Introduction

Fish farming basically deals with farming of fish and other related organisms in convenient water bodies involving intervention in the rearing process to enhance production under individual or corporate ownership of the cultivated stock for commercial purpose. The fishery practices were very popular among different tribes of the State. However, fish farming was a new experience to them except the Apatani tribe, who used to practise paddy-cum-fish culture from time immemorial. The fish farming in Arunachal Pradesh was basically a Government induced programme which was initiated in 1958-59 in a very modest scale. However, with the passage of time, there was a gradual increase of private fish farms and ponds. The people are now looking forward fisheries as means of additional income and seeking more and more Government intervention. Hence, in this chapter an attempt is made to examine the constraints faced by the fish farmers in the State as well as to evaluate the Government policies regarding fisheries.

Constraints faced by the Surveyed Fish Farmers

The fishery sector is regarded as an unpopular avenue for investment as compared to agriculture and horticulture. This may be due to the fact that there are a number of constraints faced by the fish farmers in Arunachal Pradesh. The variables like climatic and altitude within the State necessitates adoption of different technologies for different areas. Secondly, the socio-economic condition of the people makes it difficult for introduction of modern technology and practice of commercial fish farming. High rainfall and perennial problem of floods and under-utilization of aquatic resources in low lying areas of foothills of the State, non-availability of standard quality seeds in right season and inadequacy of technology transfer, insufficient rearing tank area in seed production farms for raising fingerlings have accentuated the problem of increasing the productivity. Scientific methods of fish farming have been introduced on a very limited scale. Finally, no comprehensive programme for utilization of substantially large water area for development of pisciculture has been taken up in the State due to paucity of fund (Government of Arunachal Pradesh, 2006).

The limited adoption of modern practices and low level of productivity in the surveyed fish ponds were due to a number of constraints faced by the fish farmers. In order to examine the constraints faced by the fish farmers in the surveyed ponds they were asked through an open-ended questionnaire to indicate five major constraints as per their order of preference. According to them these constraints were responsible for low level of productivity and low level of adoption of new practices. The constraints were ranked 1, 2, 3, 4 and 5 and the scores were assigned 5, 4, 3, 2 and 1 respectively on the basis of ranks. The total rank score for each constraint was obtained by multiplying the frequency with their respective score. From Chapter Five it was observed that the relationship between various variables and productivity was significantly different in the two surveyed districts. Further, these two districts are located in two agro-climatic zones. So, the constraints were also calculated separately for Lohit and Lower Subansiri district. The constraints reported by the surveyed fish farmers in the Lohit district are given in Table 6.1.

Table 6.1 shows that 'non-availability of adequate financial assistance in time' was the major problem faced by the surveyed fish farmers in Lohit district; followed by 'problem of poaching', 'inefficient marketing structure', 'poor quality of fish seed' and 'damage of ponds due to flood and excessive rain' with respective scores of 826, 589, 429, 420 and 287 respectively. It was interesting to observe that damage of ponds due to flood and excessive rain was one of the major problems in the Lohit district. The problem of flash flood is quite frequent in the surveyed area of Namsai-Chongkham block.

Table 6.1: Major Constraints reported in Lower Subansiri District

Identified Problem Areas	*Rank (Total Score)*
Non-availability of adequate financial assistance in time	1 *(826)*
Problem of poaching/ stealing/ theft of fish	2 *(589)*
Inefficient marketing structure	3 *(429)*
Poor and erratic/ inadequate supply of fish seed (fingerling)	4 *(420)*
Damage of ponds due to flood and excessive rain	5 *(287)*
High cost or adulteration of fish feed	6 *(189)*
Multiple ownership and absentee ownership	7 *(102)*
Lack of knowledge, training and know how	8 *(83)*
Problem of mortality	9 *(50)*
Other problems	10 *(25)*

Note: Figures in the parentheses indicate the respective total score.

Source: Compiled from Field Data, 2010-2012.

The constraints reported by the surveyed fish farmers in the Lower Subansiri district are given in Table 6.2.

Table 6.2: Major Constraints reported in Lower Subansiri District

Identified Problem Areas	*Rank (Total Score)*
Non-availability of adequate financial assistance in time	1 *(398)*
Inefficient marketing structure	2 *(243)*
High cost and adulteration of fish feed	3 *(198)*
Problem of poaching/stealing/theft of fish	4 *(175)*
Poor and erratic/inadequate supply of fish seed (fingerling)	5 *(150)*
Lack of knowledge, training and know how	6 *(120)*
Problem of mortality	7 *(100)*
Problem of multiple ownership and absentee ownership	8 *(89)*
Lack of skilled labour	9 *(20)*
Other problems	10 *(16)*

Note: Figures in the parentheses indicate the respective total score.

Source: Compiled from Field Data, 2010-2012.

Table 6.2 shows that 'non-availability of adequate financial assistance in time' with score of 398 was the major constraints in the Lower Subansiri also. Other constraints reported in the surveyed district were 'inefficient marketing structure', 'high cost and adulteration of fish feed', 'problem of poaching' and 'poor quality of fish seed' with the sores of 243, 198, 175 and 150 respectively.

In order to get a clear picture, a detailed analysis of the five major constraints on the basis of the addition of the total score reported by the surveyed fish farmers in the two surveyed districts were taken into account separately. These are as follows:

1. Non-availability of adequate financial assistance in time,
2. Problem of Poaching,
3. Inefficient Marketing Structure,
4. Poor and inadequate supply of fish seed, and
5. High cost and adulteration of fish feed .

The details were shown in Table 6.3, 6.4, 6.5, 6.6 and 6.7 respectively.

Problem of Finance

Problem of finance was the major problem for fish farmers in the small scale fishery sector in India. Most of them are very poor and the most marginalized communities in the society. Their low social status is a result of poverty as well as exploitation by middlemen and merchants. The middlemen have control over credit and fish marketing, which drains away the surplus generated and often make them indebted.

In both the surveyed districts, the problem of finance emerged as the major problem 159 fish farmers out of the 280 fish farmers (56.79 per cent) ranked it as first constraint in adoption of new technology and low level of productivity. In Lohit district 106 fish farmers (56.38 per cent) reported it as the main problem. On the other hand, 53 fish farmers (56.79 per cent) in the Lower Subansiri reported it as the major obstacles faced by them. The details were given in Table 6.3.

Table 6.3: Non-availability of Adequate Financial Assistance

Rank	Lohit		Lower Subansiri		Total	
	Nos.	Score	Nos.	Score	Nos.	Score
I	106 (56.38)	530	53 (57.61)	265	159 (56.79)	795
II	62 (32.98)	248	21 (22.83)	84	83 (29.64)	332
III	9 (4.79)	27	15 (16.30)	45	24 (8.57)	72
IV	10 (5.32)	20	1 (1.09)	2	11 (3.93)	22
V	1 (0.53)	1	2 (2.17)	2	3 (1.07)	3
Total	188	826	92	398	280	1224

Note: Figures in the parentheses indicate the percentage of the total.
Source: Compiled from Field Data, 2010-2012.

Problem of Poaching

Another main problem faced by the fish farmers in the study area was poaching. Poaching is considered as a major inhabiting factor. It arises because ponds are situated at varying distance between each other and far from fish farmer's house. The problem was high in the surveyed area of Lohit district, where as many as 189 fish farmers reported about the problem. The intensity of this problem was less in Lower Subansiri district 44 fish farmers reported about the problem. This is because the average distance of fish farmer's house from pond in Lohit district was higher than that of Lower Subansiri district. The details were given in Table 6.4.

Table 6.4: Problem of Poaching

Rank	Lohit		Lower Subansiri		Total	
	Nos.	Score	Nos.	Score	Nos.	Score
I	15 (7.94)	75	15 (34.09)	75	30 (12.88)	150
II	50 (26.46)	200	20 (45.45)	80	70 (30.04)	280
III	89 (47.09)	267	3 (6.82)	9	92 (39.48)	276
IV	12 (6.35)	24	5 (11.36)	10	17 (7.30)	34
V	23 (12.17)	23	1 (2.27)	1	24 (10.30)	24
Total	189	589	44	175	233	764

Note: Figures in the parentheses indicate the percentage of the total.
Source: Compiled from Field Data, 2010–2012.

Fish farmers try to tackle poaching in various ways. In case of Lohit district the large pond owners prevent poaching by hiring security for the ponds or by settling migrant fishermen near the pond. He takes care of the day to day management of the ponds as well as guards it from poachers.

Problem of Inefficient Marketing Structure

The problem of inefficient marketing structure was another major problem in both the surveyed districts. A total of 207 fish farmers reported about the problem with total score of 672. The details were given in Table 6.5.

In fact, in earlier chapter, it was observed that the Channel-I i.e., producer → retailer → consumer was the most popular and the marketing margin was the highest and producer's share in consumer's rupee was the lowest in Channel-I. This happens to those fish farmers who were not close to road and as a result they highly depend on retailers, i.e., middlemen.

Table 6.5: Inefficient Marketing Structure

Rank	*Lohit*		*Lower Subansiri*		*Total*	
	Nos.	*Score*	*Nos.*	*Score*	*Nos.*	*Score*
I	20 (17.09)	100	14 (15.56)	70	34 (16.43)	170
II	66 (56.41)	264	12 (13.33)	48	78 (37.68)	312
III	9 (7.69)	27	16 (17.78)	48	25 (12.08)	75
IV	16 (13.68)	32	29 (32.22)	58	45 (21.74)	90
V	6 (5.13)	6	19 (21.11)	19	25 (12.08)	25
Total	117	429	90	243	207	672

Note: Figures in the parentheses indicate the percentage of the total.

Source: Compiled from Field Data, 2010-2012.

Problem of Poor Quality and Inadequate Supply of Fish Seed

Another problem faced by the fish farmer is the low quality of fish seed. As many as 192 fish farmer reported about this problem. In case of Lohit district alone the number was 152 with the total score of 420. The details are given in Table 6.6

Table 6.6: Poor and Inadequate Supply of Fish Seeds

Rank	*Lohit*		*Lower Subansiri*		*Total*	
	Nos.	*Score*	*Nos.*	*Score*	*Nos.*	*Score*
I	33 (21.71)	165	9 (22.50)	45	42 (21.88)	210
II	12 (7.89)	48	19 (47.50)	76	31 (16.15)	124
III	20 (13.16)	60	5 (12.50)	15	25 (13.02)	75
IV	60 (39.47)	120	7 (17.50)	14	67 (34.90)	134
V	27 (17.76)	27	0 (0.00)	0	27 (14.06)	27
Total	152	420	40	150	192	570

Note: Figures in the parentheses indicate the percentage of the total.
Source: Compiled from Field Data, 2010–2012.

Stocking high quality and healthy seed is fundamental to success for fish farming. The small size pond owners find it a difficult task to procure good quality of fish seed. It was interesting to observe that in many cases fish seed purchased from market were found to be tadpole instead of fish seed. This problem was found to be quite high in the surveyed area of Lohit district.

Problem of High Cost and Adulteration of Fish Feed

Finally, an attempt was also made for the problem of high cost and adulteration of fish feed. It was found that total of 117 fish farmers reported about the problem with the total score of 387. The problem was quite high in Lower Subansiri district with 69 fish farmers reported about the problem with total score of 198. The details were given in Table 6.7.

In view of above mentioned constraints as perceived by surveyed fish farmers, it will be quite interesting to examine the State Government policy towards the fishery sector; which was discussed below in Section "Role of Government in Fishery Development."

Table 6.7: High Cost and Adulteration of Fish Feed

Rank	*Lohit*		*Lower Subansiri*		*Total*	
	Nos.	*Score*	*Nos.*	*Score*	*Nos.*	*Score*
I	22 (45.83)	110	6 (8.70)	30	28 (23.93)	140
II	9 (18.75)	36	19 (27.54)	76	28 (23.93)	112
III	12 (25.00)	36	14 (20.29)	42	26 (22.22)	78
IV	2 (4.17)	4	20 (28.99)	40	22 (18.80)	44
V	3 (6.25)	3	10 (14.49)	10	13 (11.11)	13
Total	48	189	69	198	117	387

Note: Figures in the parentheses indicate the percentage of the total.
Source: Compiled from Field Data, 2010-2012.

Role of Government in Fishery Development

There was no specific planning for development of fisheries in Arunachal Pradesh. However, allocation was made in fishery sector since during Second Five Year Plan onwards. If we compare the outlay to the fishery sector with total State plan outlay during various plan period, it was found that State plan outlay increased from ₹509.00 lakh in Second Five Year Plan to ₹8,79,055.00 lakh in Eleventh Five Year Plan. Although, there was absolute increase in outlay in fishery sector but in percentage term outlay for fishery to total State plan outlay remained less than 1 per cent during all the Five Year Plan, with maximum allocation during Fourth Five Year Plan period (0.67 per cent). The details were shown in Table 6.8.

Now an attempt was made to analyse the expenditure pattern of the State Government during 1991-92 to 2009-10. In the period of nineteen years the total expenditure of the State Government increased by eleven times, whereas the outlay in the fishery sector increased by eight times. The expenditure in the fishery sector as a percentage of expenditure in agriculture and allied sector was ranging from 3.2 per cent in 2002.03 to 1.4 per cent in 2007-08. On the other hand the expenditure in fishery sector as percentage of total Government expenditure remained below 0.5 per cent throughout the period. The details were given in Table 6.9.

Table 6.8: Financial Allocation to the Fishery Sector of Arunachal Pradesh during Various Plan Periods

(in ₹ lakh)

Period	*State Plan Outlay*	*Outlay for Fisheries*	*Percentage of Allocation*
1st FY Plan (1950–1956)	NA	NA	NA
2nd FY Plan (1956–1961)	509.00	1.00	0.17
3rd FY Plan (1961–1966)	715.00	1.70	0.24
Annual Plan (1966–1969)	874.15	2.90	0.33
4th FY Plan (1969–1974)	1799.00	12.00	0.67
5th FY Plan (1974–1978)	633.00	3.83	0.61
Annual Plan (1978–1980)	4681.00	10.00	0.21
6th FY Plan (1980–1985)	22290.00	114.20	0.51
7th FY Plan (1985–1990)	55561.00	252.45	0.45
Annual Plan (1990–1992)	38656.00	172.00	0.45
8th FY Plan (1992–1997)	179153.00	734.00	0.41
9th FY Plan (1997–2002)	356989.00	904.17	0.25
10th FY Plan (2002–2007)	388832.00	2394.00	0.62
11th FY Plan (2007–2012)	879055.00	3886.00	0.44

Source: Department of Planning, Government of Arunachal Pradesh.

Table 6.9: Expenditure of State Government during 1991-92 to 2009-10

(in ₹ lakh)

Year	*Fishery*	*Agriculture and Allied*	*Total Expenditure*	*Fishery as Percentage of*	
				Agriculture and Allied	*Total Expenditure*
1	2	3	4	5	6
1991-92	162.20	6498.60	42414.40	2.50	0.38
1992-93	197.06	8072.98	49234.80	2.44	0.40
1993-94	228.01	10354.30	56176.30	2.20	0.41
1994-95	238.24	10053.54	67868.50	2.37	0.35
1995-96	270.08	12022.06	79352.50	2.25	0.34
1996-97	312.94	12020.88	87915.60	2.60	0.36
1997-98	322.14	13435.34	95846.20	2.40	0.34
1998-99	300.95	13670.64	98494.70	2.20	0.31
1999-00	312.49	13874.80	118112.00	2.25	0.26
2000-01	332.83	12486.65	127130.00	2.67	0.26
2001-02	402.57	15019.32	133232.00	2.68	0.30
2002-03	450.83	14101.08	132145.00	3.20	0.34

(Contd...)

Table 6.9: *(Contd...)*

1	2	3	4	5	6
2003-04	529.31	21480.25	182525.00	2.46	0.29
2004-05	452.98	18439.04	188471.00	2.46	0.24
2005-06	527.59	22699.60	210526.21	2.32	0.25
2006-07	490.89	24167.21	248283.46	2.03	0.20
2007-08	659.43	47077.84	298661.90	1.40	0.22
2008-09	887.15	35075.43	416188.59	2.53	0.21
2009-10	1369.76	46157.91	479271.85	2.97	0.29

Source: Annual Financial Statement of Arunachal Pradesh (different Issues), Department of Finance, Government of Arunachal Pradesh.

It was interesting to observe that the revenue expenditure in the fishery sector was quite high throughout the period. During 1991-92 to 2009-10 total expenditure incurred in the fishery sector was ₹8,447.45 lakh out of which ₹8,049.25 (95.29 per cent) was revenue expenditure and capital expenditure was only ₹398.20 lakh (4.71 per cent) against the national average of 8.51 per cent (Appendix IV). The share of revenue expenditure was as high as 99.56 per cent during 2004-05, which shows that almost nothing was kept for capital component in that particular year. The details were given in Table 6.10.

Table 6.10: Composition of Revenue Expenditure and Capital Expenditure to the Total Expenditure in Fishery by State Government during 1991-92 to 2009-10

(in ₹ lakh)

Year	*Expenditure in Fishery Sector*		
	Revenue	*Capital*	*Total*
1	2	3	4
1991-92	144.20 (88.90)	18.00 (11.10)	162.20
1992-93	177.36 (90.00)	19.70 (10.00)	197.06
1993-94	207.38 (90.95)	20.63 (9.05)	228.01
1994-95	216.24 (90.77)	22.00 (9.23)	238.24
1995-96	262.54 (97.21)	7.54 (2.79)	270.08
1996-97	278.05 (88.85)	34.89 (11.15)	312.94
1997-98	311.11 (96.58)	11.03 (3.42)	322.14
1998-99	293.94 (97.67)	7.01 (2.33)	300.95
1999-00	303.46 (97.11)	9.03 (2.89)	312.49
2000-01	330.35 (99.25)	2.48 (0.75)	332.83

(Contd...)

Table 6.10: *(Contd...)*

1	2	3	4
2001-02	394.99 (98.12)	7.58 (1.88)	402.57
2002-03	439.45 (97.48)	11.38 (2.52)	450.83
2003-04	522.01 (98.62)	7.30 (1.38)	529.31
2004-05	450.98 (99.56)	2.00 (0.44)	452.98
2005-06	488.61 (92.61)	38.98 (7.39)	527.59
2006-07	458.89 (93.48)	32.00 (6.52)	490.89
2007-08	637.53 (96.68)	21.90 (3.32)	659.43
2008-09	862.15 (97.18)	25.00 (2.82)	887.15
2009-10	1270.01 (92.72)	99.75 (7.28)	1369.76
Total	8049.25 (95.29)	398.20 (4.71)	8447.45

Note: Figures in the parentheses indicate the percentage of total.
Source: Annual Financial Statement of Arunachal Pradesh (different Issues), Department of Finance, Government of Arunachal Pradesh.

All these expenditure were basically made for strengthening the Fishery Department of the State government in terms of manpower particularly by incurring the revenue expenditure. As a result, the State Fishery Department possessed infrastructure of 35.69 hectares of fish farm and 107.00 hectares of Beels and Lakes till 2010-11. There were only 6 numbers of hatcheries in the State during 2010-11. The details were given in Table 6.11.

Table 6.11: Fishery Infrastructure in the State of Arunachal Pradesh during 2004-05 to 2010-11

Year	*Government*		*Private*		*Hatcheries (in Nos.)*	*Area under Paddy-cum-Fish Culture*	*Finger-lings distri-buted (in, '000 Nos.)*
	Fish Farms (in ha.)	*Beels/ Lakes (in ha.)*	*Fish Ponds/ Farms (in ha.)*	*Beels/ Lakes (in ha.)*			
2004-05	31.00	99.00	1011.00	8.00	11	1171.00	9000
2005-06	55.00	99.00	6105.00	8.00	11	1171.00	9500
2006-07	35.69	128.80	1100.00	0.00	11	1200.00	10000
2007-08	35.69	128.80	1146.00	0.00	11	1305.00	11000
2008-09	35.69	107.00	9070.00	0.00	6	1325.00	10000
2009-10	30.00	107.00	6377.00	0.00	6	1345.00	12000
2010-11	35.69	107.00	9200.00	0.00	6	1375.00	11000

Source: Statistical Abstract of Arunachal Pradesh, 2011, Directorate of Economics and Statistics, Government of Arunachal Pradesh.

Central Sector Schemes and Centrally Sponsored Schemes in the Fishery Sector

During the Tenth Five Year Plan, specific schemes in fishery sector were launched under the central sector schemes and centrally sponsored schemes in the fishery sector. The Tenth Plan focused on an integrated approach to sustainable development of aquaculture and aimed at optimization of production and productivity and conservation of fishery resources, streamlining marketing arrangements and transfer of technology to farmers for increasing production. Central sector schemes and centrally sponsored schemes are based on the following objectives:

1. Enhancement of inland fish production and fish productivity,
2. Popularization of modern fish farming,
3. Creation of employment opportunities through fisheries,
4. Diversifying aquaculture practices,
5. Providing assistance to fish farmers engaged in aquaculture, and
6. Provide training to fish farmers of Fish Farmers' Development Agencies (FFDAs) and Brackish water Fish Farmer Development Agency (BFDA).

Six of the schemes, i.e., Development of Freshwater Aquaculture, Fishery Extension, Coldwater Aquaculture, Fishermen Welfare Schemes, Post-Harvest Infrastructure and Strengthening of Database Information and Networking were analysed for the period of Tenth and Eleventh Five Year Plan Periods. Two of the schemes, i.e., Post-Harvest Infrastructure and Strengthening of Database Information and Networking were having 100 per cent central share and rest of the four schemes, i.e., Development of Freshwater Aquaculture, Fishery Extension, Coldwater Aquaculture and Fishermen Welfare Schemes had State's matching grant. The details were given in Table 6.12.

Table 6.12 shows that among central sector schemes and centrally sponsored schemes, the highest allocation was made.

Table 6.12: Central Sector Schemes and Centrally Sponsored Schemes for Fisheries in Arunachal Pradesh during Tenth and Eleventh Five Year Plans

(in ₹ lakh)

Name of Schemes		*DFA*	*FE*	*CA*	*FWS*	*PHI*	*SDIN*
Funding Pattern	Central Share	75.00	80.00	75.00	50.00	100.00	100.00
	State Share	25.00	20.00	25.00	50.00	0	0
Tenth Plan Outlay	Central Share	300.00	16.00	9.83	32.00	100.00	40.65
	State Share	100.00	4.00	3.28	32.00	—	—
	Total	400.00	20.00	13.11	64.00	100.00	40.65
TenthPlanExpenditure	Central Share	142.37 (47.46)	5.72 (35.75)	241.15 (2453.20)	64.00 (200.00)	100.00 (100.00)	40.65 (100.00)
	State Share Expenditure	(63.50)	63.50 (35.75)	1.43 (221.95)	7.28 (200.00)	64.00 —	—
	Total	205.87 (51.47)	7.15 (35.75)	248.43 (1894.97)	128.00 (200.00)	100.00 (100.00)	40.65 (100.00)
Eleventh Plan Outlay	Central Share	303.00	9.60	45.00	160.00	100.00	50.00
	State Share	101.00	2.40	15.00	160.00	—	—
	Total	404.00	12.00	60.00	320.00	100.00	50.00

Note: Figures in the parentheses indicate expenditure as percentage of outlay for respective component.

DFA: Development of Freshwater Aquaculture, FE: Fishery Extension, CA: Coldwater Aquaculture, FWS: Fishermen Welfare Schemes,
PHI: Post-Harvest Infrastructure, and SDIN: Strengthening of Database Information and Networking.

Source: Planning Department, Government of Arunachal Pradesh, Itanagar.

during Tenth Five Year Plan in development of freshwater aquaculture, i.e., ₹ 400.00 lakh but the State was able to spend only ₹ 205.87 lakh, i.e., 51.47 per cent. On the other hand, the allocation made in the coldwater fisheries was amounting to only ₹13.11 lakh, but the expenditure incurred was as high as ₹248.43 lakh. So the expenditure pattern during the Tenth Five Year Plan showed that high priority was given to coldwater fisheries including Trout in high altitude area. There is no doubt that there is tremendous potential for coldwater fisheries in Arunachal Pradesh but it contributes around 15 per cent of the total fish production of the State (Das, 2008). The expenditure under schemes with 100 per cent central share, i.e., Post-Harvest Infrastructure and Strengthening of Database Information and Networking were found to be fully utilized.

In case of central sector scheme and central sponsored schemes in the North Eastern region of India during Eleventh Five Year Plan, the allocation share to Nagaland was highest, i.e., 22.76 per cent followed by Arunachal Pradesh and Assam with the share of 22.42 per cent and 10.88 per cent respectively. On the other hand the share to the State of Meghalaya was only 0.50 per cent. The details were given in Figure 6.1.

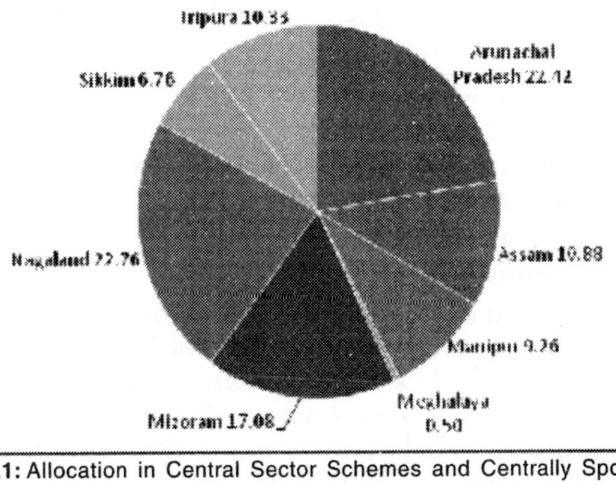

Fig. 6.1: Allocation in Central Sector Schemes and Centrally Sponsored Schemes for Fisheries among different States of North Eastern Region of India during Eleventh Five Year Plan *(in per cent)*

Source: http://www.dahd.nic.in

Achievements of Fish Farmers Development Agency in Arunachal Pradesh

The Fish Farmers Development Agency (FFDA) scheme was initiated as a pilot project by the Department of Agriculture and Corporation, Government of India in 1974-75 in some States of the country in order to utilize village tanks and ponds for the purpose of aquaculture by setting up district level agencies. The scheme was introduced to more States and thus, the number of agencies also increased. FFDAs are provided with necessary funds, Extension of Service Units and required infrastructure so as to develop freshwater fish culture in each district. The FFDAs used to enjoy reasonable autonomy in their operations. The specific objectives of the FFDA scheme are:

1. To facilitate leasing of water bodies owned by local bodies to farmers/groups.
2. To reclaim the water bodies and to bring all the suitable water areas under the scheme.
3. To organize the work of the Agency in such a way that it serves as a nucleus activity for spreading to other areas.
4. To create a new array of fish farmers by imparting necessary training and supply of input.
5. To popularize the new avocation and provide increased employment opportunities to rural mass.
6. To contribute for improving rural economy by making fish farming economically viable.

The functions of FFDA can be explained with the help of the following Figure (Figure 6.2):

According to data provided by the Ministry of Agriculture, Government of India the FFDAs was successful in bringing some of the derelict/semi-derelict water bodies. In North East India, 53 FFDAs were operating but in Arunachal Pradesh only two FFDAs were functioning with the area covered by 926 ha. The number of beneficiaries by the two FFDA was 5689 and 3840 persons received training from the agency. The details were given in Table 6.13.

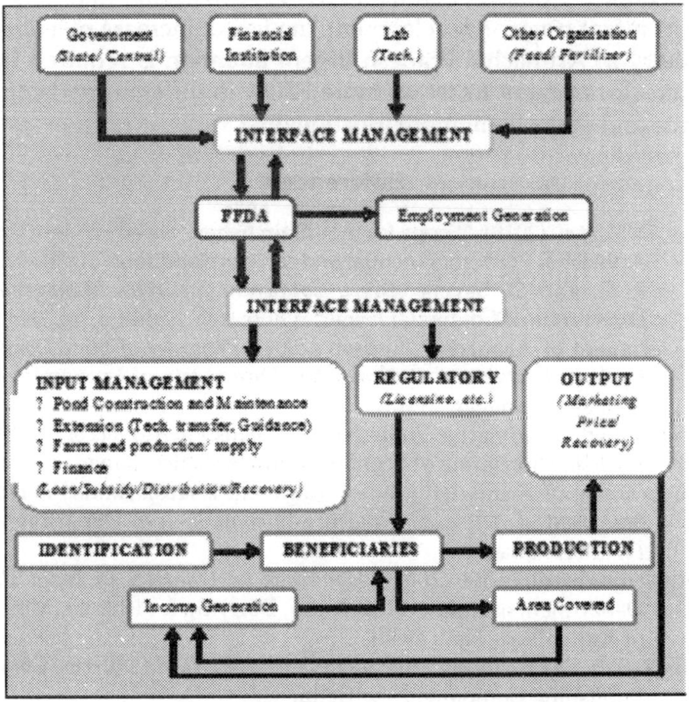

Fig. 6.2: Functions of Fish Farmers Development Agency (FFDA)

Source: Misra, S.R., *Inland Fisheries in India : Issues and Concerns,* Concept Publishing Company, 2006, p. 73.

Table 6.13: Achievements of Fish Farmers Development Agencies in North Eastern Region of India till 2005-06

	Arunachal Pradesh	*NER*	*India*
No. of FFDAs	2	53	429
Water Area Covered *(in ha.)*	926	27210	697790
Water Area Covered *(in ha.)*/ FFDA	463.00	513.40	1626.55
No. of Fish Farmer Trained	3840	162302	825187
No. of Fish Farmer Trained/ FFDA	1920.00	3062.30	1923.51
No. of Beneficiaries	5689	114736	1204228
No. of Beneficiaries/ FFDA	2844.50	2164.83	2807.06

Source: Hand Book on Fisheries Statistics 2006, Department of Animal Husbandry, Dairying and Fisheries, Ministry of Agriculture, Government of India.

Table 6.13 shows that the FFDA in Arunachal Pradesh is still in its infant stage of development. In view of increase potential of fishery in Arunachal Pradesh urgent attention is required from State Government to set up more FFDA in different parts of the State and make them more functional.

References

Das, D. N. *et al.* (2010): "Scope for mountain fishery based eco-tourism in Arunachal Pradesh: Potential and recommendations", in Mahanta, P. C. and D. Sarma (eds.), *Coldwater Fisheries Management*, Directorate of Coldwater Fisheries Research, Nainital, pp. 285-296.

Government of Arunachal Pradesh (2006): *Estimates of State Domestic Product of Arunachal Pradesh 2006*, Directorate of Economics and Statistics, Itanagar.

Government of Arunachal Pradesh (2011): *Statistical Abstract of Arunachal Pradesh*, Directorate of Economics and Statistics, Itanagar.

Government of Arunachal Pradesh (different Issues): *Annual Financial Statement of Arunachal Pradesh (different Issues)*, Department of Finance, Itanagar.

Government of India (2007): *Handbook on Fisheries in India 2006*, Department of Animal Husbandry, Dairying & Fisheries, Ministry of Agriculture, New Delhi.

Misra, S. R. (2006): *Inland Fisheries in India: Issues and Concerns*, Concept Publishing Company, New Delhi.

Chapter - 7

Principal Findings and Policy Implications

Introduction

The primary interest of any empirical study lies in extracting policy implications for addressing the opportunities and challenges identified during the process of investigation. Altogether, there is ample scope for fishery development in the State, but this sector is plagued by a number of challenges which act as impediments in its growth process. This chapter is the concluding chapter, and as such this chapter recapitulates the principal findings of the study and enumerates the broad references regarding trends and patterns of production of fishes, its productivity, resource-use efficiency as well as its marketing structure in the State. The important policy recommendations based on findings are then presented for improving the performance of fishery sector of the State.

Principal Findings

Principal Findings from the Analysis of Secondary Data

The principal findings from the analysis of secondary data are as follows:

1. The world's fish production increased from19.75 million tonnes in 1950 to 140.47 million tonnes in 2004 (i.e., 7.1 times increase). On the other hand, India's fish production has increased 6.08 million tonnes in 2004 from a mere 0.73 million tonnes in 1950 (i.e., 8.3 times increase). As a result, the share of India in global fish production increased from 2.60 per cent in 1965 to 4.33

per cent in 2004. It shows that growth in fish production in India was at a faster rate than that of the world which was mainly due to increasing contribution from inland fisheries and aquaculture.

2. The average annual exponential growth rate for inland fish production of India was found to be 2.5 per cent with 0.01 per cent level of significance during the period of 1990-91 to 2010-11. Thus, India's fisheries constituted an important sector of our national economy for various reasons. One of the important reasons is its increasing contribution to our Gross Domestic Product (GDP). Its contribution to agricultural sector increased form 1.46 per cent to 4.93 per cent during 1970-71 to 2010-11.
3. The North Eastern Region has vast untapped potential for fisheries in terms of many rivers, streams, floodplain wetlands, lakes, ponds and large areas under rice fish culture system. The region consists of only around 8 per cent of total area of the country but it contains 9.58 per cent of rivers and canals, 19.92 per cent of flood plains lakes and derelict water and 15.37 per cent of tanks and ponds of the country. In fact, North East India is considered as one of the hot spots of freshwater fish biodiversity in the world. This water resource harbours 258 fish species belonging to 21 families and 76 genera (Mahanta, 2010). The literature reveals that efforts were being made to assess the rice fish germplasm resources available in this region with respect to commercial utilization. With growing demand for consumption, aquarium and sports, it is necessary to evaluate potential species on the basis of different criteria.
4. A study reveals that accordingly to preliminary evaluation, out of 186 fish species 62 (33.33 per cent) were considered as only food fish followed by 53 (28.44 per cent) as only ornamental. The rest were food as well as ornamental (12.90 per cent), sports as well as ornamental (9.67 per cent), etc. (NEDFi Data Bank, 2007). So far economic value is concerned, it is evaluated that out of the 186 species, 34 fish species have market demand better than Indian major carp whereas 19

species have similar economic values. This indicates that there is great potential for fresh water fisheries in the States of North East India through culture of indigenous fish species. In addition to it, in this region of the country, the fish is traditionally raised along with paddy or rain fed low lands (both shallow and deep water). In many areas, irrigation fed rice fields have also been adapted locally by the farmers to include fish farming (Das, 2002).

5. Arunachal Pradesh, our study area, is located in the extreme north eastern corner of India. The State is well endowed for inland water fisheries. It is situated in the monsoon belt. It received an average annual rainfall of around 2721.80 mm (Statistical Abstract of Arunachal Pradesh, 2011). In fact, Arunachal Pradesh consists of around 31.94 per cent of the total area of the North Eastern Region of India but it contains 26.42 per cent of flood plain, lakes and derelict water, 74.39 per cent of tanks and ponds and 56.48 per cent of total water bodies of the region. Thus, the State has enormous potential for development of fisheries in the region. In fact, fish from time immemorial has been an important dietary food of the people of the State. In addition, paddy-cum-fish cultivation is an important component of fisheries in general, and culture fisheries in particular, of the State. The best example of the paddy-cum-fish culture of the State is the Apatani plateau of Lower Subansiri district. There was not much reliable data regarding the extent of area of paddy-cum-fish cultivation in the State. According to one study (Das, 2002) the rice fish culture area consisted of around 53.51 per cent of culture fisheries area. Lower Subansiri district alone (87.38 per cent) had the highest percentage of paddy-cum-fish cultivation among all the districts of Arunachal Pradesh. The contribution of other districts was insignificant. In fact, recently rice-cum-fish-cum duck cultivation is growing popular in Lohit district (*The Arunachal Times*, 14th September, 2012). According to another estimate (Moda, 2005) paddy field consisted of 40.04 per cent of total fisheries in the State.

6. The fisheries programme was first initiated in the year

1958-59 in a very modest scale. However, with the passage of time and expansion of fisheries development activities, pisciculture has taken a firm root in the State. The people are presently looking forward to fisheries as a means of additional income and seeking more and more Government intervention for this purpose.

7. Fish production in Arunachal Pradesh increased from 1,250 tonnes in 1991-92 to 3040 tonnes in 2010-11 (i.e., 2.4 times). But there is significant inter-district variation of production of fishes in Arunachal Pradesh. It is found that Lohit district (13.22 per cent) topped the production of fishes followed by Changlang (9.26 per cent). It is clear that the fish production is more in relatively foothills districts adjoining Assam borders. On the other hand, the fish production is less in hilly districts of the State in spite of the fact that there is so much scope for development of cold water fisheries in those hilly districts. The only exception was Lower Subansiri district where traditional paddy-cum-fish cultivation was very popular among the Apatani tribe of Ziro valley of Lower Subansiri district.
8. From the evaluation of State Government's policy towards fishery it was found that, in the period of nineteen years (1991-92 to 2009-10) the total expenditure of the State Government increased by eleven times, whereas the outlay in the fishery sector increased by eight times. The expenditure in the fishery sector as a percentage of expenditure in agriculture and allied sector was ranging from 3.2 per cent in 2002.03 to 1.4 per cent in 2007-08. On the other hand the expenditure in fishery sector as percentage of total Government expenditure remained below 0.5 per cent throughout the period.
9. It was interesting to observe that the revenue expenditure in the fishery sector was quite high throughout the period. During 1991-92 to 2009-10 total expenditure increased in the fishery sector was ₹8,447.45 lakh out of which ₹8,049.25 (95.29 per cent) was revenue expenditure and capital expenditure was only ₹398.20 lakh

(4.71 per cent) against the national average of 8.51 per cent. The share of revenue expenditure was as high as 99.56 per cent during 2004-05, which shows that almost nothing was kept for capital component in that particular year. All these expenditure were basically made for strengthening the Fishery Department of the State government in terms of manpower particularly by incurring the revenue expenditure.

10. During the Tenth Five Year Plan, specific schemes in fishery sector were launched under the central sector schemes and centrally sponsored schemes in the fishery sector. The Tenth Plan focused on an integrated approach to sustainable development of aquaculture and aimed at optimization of production and productivity and conservation of fishery resources, streamlining marketing arrangements and transfer of technology to farmers for increasing production.

11. Among central sector schemes and centrally sponsored schemes, the highest allocation was made during Tenth Five Year Plan in development of freshwater aquaculture i.e., ₹400.00 lakh but the Sate was able to spend only ₹205.87 lakh, i.e., 51.47 per cent. On the other hand, the allocation made in the Coldwater Fisheries was amounting to only ₹13.11 lakh, but the expenditure incurred was as high as ₹248.43 lakh. So the expenditure pattern during the Tenth Five Year Plan showed that high priority was given to coldwater fisheries including Trout in high altitude area. There is no doubt that there is tremendous potential for coldwater fisheries in Arunachal Pradesh but it contributes around 15 per cent of the total fish production of the State (Das, 2008). The expenditure under schemes with 100 per cent central share, i.e., Post-Harvest Infrastructure and Strengthening of Database Information and Networking were found to be fully utilized.

12. In North East India, 53 FFDAs were operating but in Arunachal Pradesh only two FFDAs were functioning with the area covered by 926 ha. The number of beneficiaries by the two FFDA was 5,689 and 3,840

persons received training from the agency.

Principal Findings from Primary Data

The principal findings from the analysis of primary data are as follows:

1. The field survey has highlighted that in both the districts more than 60 per cent of the fish farmers belonged to matured age category, i.e., 30-50 years. Around 31 per cent belonged to old age category, i.e., more than 50 years, only 8 per cent of fish farmers were young. It was observed that in Lohit district the average age of fish farmers was found to be higher, i.e., 49 years than that of Lower Subansiri district (42 years). It may be due to the fact that in Lohit district, a good number of ponds were found to be relatively large and also the matured fish farmers were found operating large size ponds since they had long experience and more managerial skill in fish production.
2. An analysis of the educational base of the sampled fish farmers showed that the overall education level of fish farmers was very low. Most of the fish farmers were illiterates (34.67 per cent). The number of illiterate fish farmers in case of Lohit district (39.50 per cent) was higher than that of Lower Subansiri district (25.00 per cent). It was also observed that only 8.33 per cent of the fish farmers were graduate and above.
3. It was found that 15.67 per cent of surveyed fish farmers had small family, 53.00 per cent had medium family and 31.33 per cent had large family. It was also observed that 34.00 per cent of fish farmers in Lohit district had large family size. This may be due to the fact that in Lohit district the size of pond was relatively big.
4. Most of the surveyed fish farmers (93.00 per cent) were male. However, it is interesting to observe that around 8.50 per cent of surveyed fish farmers were females in case of Lohit district. There was a contrasting picture regarding the gender role on the basis of fish farming

activities. The marketing activity was purely a male dominated affair in the Lohit district with 97 per cent of marketing activities were done by the males only. On the other hand, in the case of Lower Subansiri district it was found that it is purely a female activity with 100 per cent female participation in the marketing and selling of fish in the market. The preparation of pond is basically a male dominated job with contribution of 59.67 per cent. However, it was observed that in Lohit district males played a more significant role in the preparation of pond (88 per cent). Again it was observed that, in Lower Subansiri pond preparation was jointly done by both male and female (97 per cent). Feeding the fish is also an important activity where women played a more important role in both the districts. Harvesting is an activity in which both male and female were actively participating with 90.67 per cent of total contribution. It was interesting to observe that the joint contribution was found to be 100 per cent in Lower Subansiri district since it is purely a community activity.

5. The average working hours for fishing related activity is an important variable and it was found that half (50.33 per cent) of the surveyed fish farmers were engaged in fishing activity for one to two hours daily during the fishing season. However, in the case of Lower Subansiri district, it was found that more than two-third (77.00 per cent) of surveyed fish farmers were devoting more than two hours in fishing related activity.

6. The field survey also showed that the most of the surveyed fish farmers (57.00 per cent) had the experience of fish production of more than 20 years. Only 4.34 per cent of surveyed fish farmers were having fish farming experience of less than 3 years. However, in case of Lohit district it was found that 59.50 per cent of fish farmers had experience of fish production of more than 20 years.

7. Agriculture was found to be the major occupation for the respondents (80.33 per cent). In case of Lohit district, 77.00 per cent of the respondents were having agriculture as the primary occupation followed by

horticulture (7.50 per cent) and animal husbandry (5.00 per cent). But in case of Lower Subansiri district only three major types of occupation of respondents were found, i.e., agriculture (87.00 per cent), services (7.00 per cent) and business (4.00 per cent).

8. It is found that livelihood combination of agriculture and fishery has the highest share (34.67 per cent) with 32.50 per cent in Lohit district and 39.00 per cent in Lower Subansiri district. It was also observed from the survey that agriculture, horticulture, animal husbandry and fishery was the second largest combination (18.00 per cent) followed by agriculture, animal husbandry and fishery (11.50 per cent). However, in the case of Lower Subansiri district, the second most important combination is agriculture, animal husbandry and fishery (18.00 per cent) followed by agriculture, horticulture, animal husbandry and fishery (10.00 per cent). Agriculture is the most important source of income for the fish farmers, and fishery is the additional source of livelihood in the surveyed areas. It was interesting to observe that in most of the surveyed households in Lower Subansiri district, paddy-cum-fish culture was popular. It is a role model for other districts of Arunachal Pradesh. However, in Lohit district, in some of the surveyed villages, fish-cum-duck culture was found to be conducted successfully. It was found that the share of income from fishery varied from 7.16 per cent (agriculture, services and fishery combination) to 31.46 per cent (agriculture, horticulture, animal husbandry and fishery combination). It was also observed that the combination of fishery to total income was relatively more when it was combined with animal husbandry along with other combinations. It was relatively less when it was combined with services along with other combinations. This may be due to the fact that fish rearing and animal husbandry are related activity. Secondly, fish rearing is a time consuming activity which may be difficult to combine along with services.

9. On the basis of ownership of ponds it was found that most of the sampled ponds (65.36 per cent) were found to be operated by single pond owners. Relatively a small proportion of water units were owned by two or more than two owners in the study area.
10. Majority of the sampled water units were used for multipurpose activities. It was found that a major proportion of the water units were used for irrigation purposes (59.38 per cent) followed by household purpose (27.25 per cent) and then for watering and rearing of birds and animals (21.23 per cent).
11. Government Source (GS) + Market Source (MS) + Own Pond (OP) is the major combination (47.67 per cent) of fish seed collection in the study area. However, in case of Lohit district it was found that 47.50 per cent of fish seed were collected from Market Source (MS) + Own Pond (OP) combination. It was found that a major portion of fish seed were either used from own pond or collected from private hatchery.
12. The size of ponds and water bodies vary significantly in the plains and hilly districts. For example, in the surveyed plain district of Lohit, most of the ponds (64.52 per cent) consisted of medium and large size. On the other hand, in the surveyed hilly district like Lower Subansiri, most of the ponds (92.38 per cent) consisted of small category only.
13. The productivity of small size pond was found to be 506.14 kg/acre/year followed by medium size (422.13 kg/acre/year) and large size (304.54 kg/acre/year). Thus, it was observed that there was inverse relationship between the size of pond and productivity. The inverse relationship was found to be more specific in the case of Lohit district where the productivity of the small size pond was found to be 509.30 kg/acre/year whereas, the productivity of medium size pond was 416.69 kg/acre/year and that of large size pond was 304.54 kg/acre/year. On the other hand, the inverse relationship was not very specific in the case of hilly

district of Lower Subansiri where the productivity of small size pond was found to be 503.24 kg/acre/year and that of medium size pond was 490.16 kg/acre/year. The large size pond was not found in the surveyed area of Lower Subansiri district. The productivity of small size pond was much higher than that of the medium and large size pond because of the fact that the water bodies of smaller size enjoy the benefits of close supervision, intimate monitoring and sincere regulation by the family members themselves.

14. Another important observation of the surveyed pond was that there was a decline in productivity of pond as the number of shareholders increased. The productivity of sole owner pond was found to be 496.02 kg/acre/year, followed by two owners (364.97 kg/acre/year) and more than two owners (311.64 kg/acre/year). It was found that in the case of Lohit district the productivity of one owner, two owners and more than two owners pond were found to be as high as 496.32 kg/acre/year, 308.52 kg/acre/year and 254.39 kg/acre/year respectively. But it was interesting to observe that the trend is 'U'-shaped in the case of Lower Subansiri district where productivity of one owner, two owners and more than two owner ponds were found to be 502.24 kg/acre/year, 499.36 kg/acre/year and 507.26 kg/acre/year respectively. It showed that as the number of owners increased the productivity first declined in Lower Subansiri district and then it increased. However, there was a variation in the relationship of productivity and number of pond owner in the case of the surveyed districts. This variation in the two districts may be due to two factors. Firstly, Lower Subansiri is basically a hilly district and Lohit is a comparatively plain district and both the districts are from two different agro-climatic zones of the State. Secondly, in Lower Subansiri district, paddy-cum-fish culture is practiced on a very large scale.

15. An econometric analysis of sampled data helped in identifying the different variables like socio-economic

characteristics, cost of production, infrastructural facilities, etc., affecting the productivity of fish pond in both the surveyed districts. It was found that for Lohit district, eight of the estimators of the explanatory variables, i.e., gender, family size, fish seed, fish feed, manures, fertilizer, lime, etc., experience in fishery related activity, total working hours and training received have a positive sign which indicates that any increase of the eight variables would increase the productivity of fish pond. Among these eight variables five were significant at different levels. The explanatory variable like fish seed was found to be statistically significant at 0.01 levels. The variables such as experience in fishery related activity and training received were found to be statistically significant at 0.05 levels. The other variables like fish feed and family size were significant at 0.10 levels. The rest of the variables like gender, manure, fertilizer, lime, etc., and total working hours had positive coefficient but were not significant. Among fourteen explanatory variables, six variables like age, education level, pond size, distance of water bodies, distance from market and number of pond owners were found to be negatively related. It is interesting to observe that age and education were found to be negatively related but they were not significant. The variables like number of pond owners and pond size had not only negative coefficient but they were significant at 0.01 level. This means that the higher number of pond owners and the larger the pond size, the lower was the productivity from the surveyed ponds. The other variables like distance of water bodies and distance from market were not only negative but were significant at 0.05 and 0.10 levels respectively.

16. On the other hand, in Lower Subansiri district was found that twelve explanatory variables like age of the fish farmers, gender, education level, family size, fish seed, fish feed, manure, fertilizer, lime, etc., experience in fishing related activity, distance of water bodies, total working hours, training received and cultivable land

area had positive signs which indicates that any increase in any of these variables would increase the productivity of fish ponds. Among these twelve explanatory variables six were significant at different levels of probability. For example, explanatory variables of experience in fishery related activity and family size were found to be significant at 0.01 levels. The explanatory variables like fish feed and total working hours were found to be significant at 0.05 levels. The explanatory variables such as fish seed and educational level were found to be significant at 0.10 levels. The rest of the variables like manure, fertilizer, lime etc.; cultivable land area, gender of fish farmer, training received, age of fish farmers and distance of water bodies had positive coefficients but were found to be insignificant. The remaining three explanatory variables like pond size, distance from market and number of pond owners were found to be negative. However, out of these three explanatory variables, distances from market and pond size were found to be significant at 0.01 and 0.10 levels respectively.

17. An analysis of the cost of production showed that, the total cost of fish was found to be ₹50.69/kg. However, there was large variation of total cost in the different size of pond ranging from ₹57.14/kg in large pond farming to ₹44.12/kg in medium pond farming. However, out of the total cost, 71.36 per cent consisted of variable cost and the rest 28.64 per cent consisted of fixed cost. However, the fixed cost was found to be the highest among small pond owners and variable cost was found to be highest in case of larger pond owners. This may be due to the fact that large pond owners may have to use more hired labour. The total revenue of fish obtained was found to be ₹82.39/kg ranging from ₹85.21/kg in small pond owner to ₹80.00/kg in large fish farming. This gives the gross margin of ₹46.76/ kg which was high in case of medium fish farming and small fish farming with ₹48.79/kg and ₹48.75/kg respectively. It is interesting to observe that the value

of gross margin was significantly low in the case of large fish farming (₹37.54/kg). On the other hand, in the case of net return, the farmers from medium fish farming were found to be the most efficient (₹36.62/kg) as compared to small (₹32.93/kg) and large (₹22.86/kg) pond owners. This is because in case of small pond owners, the fixed cost was relatively high and in case of large pond owners, the variable cost was relatively high. Hence, the analysis shows that there was significant difference in net returns in different size of fish farming.

18. In the study area, the Benefit Cost Ratio or profitability index was found to be greater than one, i.e., 1.64 and it indicates that the fish farming is profitable in the study area. However, in order to acquire higher benefit-cost ratio, it is necessary to increase the quality of seed, feed and skilled labour. The benefit-cost ratio values were estimated to be 1.63, 1.83 and 1.40 for small, medium and large pond farmers respectively. The value shows that medium pond farmers were recovering ₹1.83 by investing one rupee whereas small and large pond farmers were recovering ₹1.63 and ₹1.40 respectively. Expense Structure Ratio (ESR) was 0.40 which implies that about 40 per cent of the total cost of production consisted of fixed cost of production. This makes the fish farming worthwhile since an increase in production with variable cost will increase the total revenue leaving the fixed cost unchanged. The expense structure ratio was higher in the case of small pond farming (0.43) followed by medium and large sized pond with 0.38 and 0.35 respectively. The Rate of Return in the study area was 0.64 which shows that for every rupee one invested paise 64 was gained by the fish farmer.

19. Cobb-Douglas production function was used for the estimation of elasticities of production and returns to scale. In case of Lohit district it was found that the independent variables included in the study affect fish production significantly. The sum of production of elasticities of all variables, i.e., fish seeds, fish feeds, manure, fertilizers, lime, etc., and labour was 1.77, which

indicates that the increasing returns to scale existed in the production of the sampled ponds. On the other hand, in case of Lower Subansiri also there was an increasing return to scale (1.88) which is higher than that of Lohit district. This indicates that in case of Lohit district the increase in one per cent of the variables will result in 1.77 per cent increase in fish production and in Lower Subansiri district it will result in 1.88 per cent increase in production. It is also clear from the analysis that the individual production elasticities of fish seeds, fish feeds, manure, fertilizers, lime, etc., and labour are not only positive, but also most of the variables are significant. However, a distinct pattern was observed in our sampled districts. For example, in case of Lohit district, the highest expected increase in fish production was observed due to increase in fish seeds (fingerlings) since the coefficient of fish seed was found to be 0.63 which is significant at 0.05 level. Hence, it can be said that in Lohit district an increase in investment in fish seed may help fish farmers to increase the fish production. However, in Lower Subansiri the most important factor of production was found to be fish feed with 0.69 production elasticity values which was significant at 0.05 level. Hence, it can be concluded that in Lower Subansiri district an increase in fish feed will help to increase fish production.

20. Marginal Value Productivities (MVPs) of all the inputs in both the districts were estimated and found to be positive. In fact, in all the cases, the values of MVPs were more than one. This explains that an investment of rupee one on any input under our study is likely to increase fish production by more than the value of rupee one. Specifically, in Lohit district an investment of rupee one in fish seed was likely to generate an additional income to the extent of ₹2.31. On the other hand, in Lower Subansiri rupee one investment in fish feed was likely to generate an additional income to the extent of ₹2.56. Of course, it largely depends also upon the price of fish.
21. An analysis of marketing structure of the surveyed districts showed that channel I, i.e., Producer → Retailer

→ Consumer (66.00 per cent) was the most popular channel followed by channel III, i.e., Producer → Consumer (23.00 per cent) and channel II, i.e., Producer → Vendor → Consumer (11.00 per cent) respectively. The channel II existed only in Lohit district among the two surveyed districts but it was the second important channel with 16.50 per cent share. It was found that the producers share in consumer's rupee varied from 64.29 per cent to 72.73 per cent in the marketing of fish through identified channels. It was found that the marketing margin was quite high particularly in channel I. A comparatively lower producer's share in consumer's rupee in channel I and channel II was mainly because of the presence of agents who corner their margins by providing services in the fish marketing. Thus, though these two parameters, namely producer's share in consumer's rupee as well as quantum of costs and margins indicate that existing system of fish marketing in the study area was by and large inefficient. In fact, it was found that marketing system was quite unorganized to a great disadvantage to the fish pond owners. The estimates of marketing efficiency of fish through various channels through Shepherd's formula. It shows that the marketing efficiency is higher in channel-II in Lohit district (10.75) and lowest in the channel-I of Lower Subansiri district (7.12).

22. Finally, a study was conducted regarding the constraints faced by the sampled fish farmers. The study showed that, in Lohit district 'non-availability of adequate financial assistance in time' was the major problem faced by the surveyed fish farmers; followed by 'problem of poaching', 'inefficient marketing structure', 'poor quality of fish seed' and 'damage of ponds due to flood and excessive rain'. It was interesting to observe that damage of ponds due to flood and excessive rain was one of the major problems in the Lohit district. The problem of flash flood is quite frequent in the surveyed area of Namsai-Chongkham block. Similarly in Lower

Subansiri district also 'non-availability of adequate financial assistance in time' was the major constraints faced by the surveyed fish farmers. Other constraints reported in the surveyed district were 'inefficient marketing structure', 'high cost and adulteration of fish feed', 'problem of poaching' and 'poor quality of fish seed'.

Policy Implications

The following policy recommendations were suggested for improving performance of fishery sector of the State:

- On the background of the existing status, the fishery sector of the State appears to be in infant stage of development in spite of its enormous potential. As the State is the owner of the fishery waters of diversified zones, the aquaculture packages of practices need to be referred for adoption in the State in accordance with the available ecological zones for proper exclusion. For example, the hilly districts of the State hold the grounds from high altitude fishery development particularly in the trout production and sports fishery. On the other hand, the flood plain fisheries of the State encompass the natural water bodies and lakes situated in the relatively plain districts where composite carp production system may be incorporated. Therefore, there is an immense scope for development of fish farming in the State to provide a source of income and employment to the people of the State. However, there is a big gap (the highest deficit among the States of North East India) between the actual production (3,040 tonnes) and the estimated annual requirement of fish (15,269 tonnes) (Appendix V). It was also found that fish farmers are not getting desired fish production in their pond due to lack of good quality of fish seed and fish feed. They have to purchase it from the market. It is imperative to popularise low cost fish farming system. Hence, *the Government should encourage public private partnership for popularising as well as augmenting the production of fishes of the State.*

- It was found that private fish farmers suffered from lack of adequate finance. The financial institution like banks are sometimes found to be hesitant to lend finance for fish culture since they are not curtain of fish farmer's repayments capacity. At the same time the number of banks is also limited in the State. *Under these circumstances, it is suggested to introduce and popularise micro credit among fish farmers through formation of self-help groups.*
- It was further observed that the fish farmers also suffer from lack of quality seeds. The seed production is an important link which should be improved first because development of aquaculture mostly depends on it. In Arunachal Pradesh, though seed production has been an increasing trend but it is unable to meet the demand of quality seed for culture ponds and tank as well as rice fields. Moreover, seed production needs skilled manpower, proper maintenance of breed fish and other related facilities, which are not still available in most of the State's fish seed farmers. *So, the condition of fish seed farm needs to be updated and standardised for maintaining optimum level of output, which calls for special research attention.*
- It was also found that most of the fish farmers are either illiterate or not much educated. They are not aware of adoption of modern practices of fish farming. *Hence, regular training, demonstration and outreach programmes should be provided to the fish farmer by the State Fishery Departments in collaborations with Krishi Vigyan Kendras.*
- The conventional fishing system is no longer able to address the grassroots level of reality. *This calls for integrated approach of fishery with agriculture and other allied sector like piggery-cum-fish culture; duck-cum-fish culture; duck-cum-fish-cum-piggery culture.* It may be noted that the role model of paddy-cum-fish culture was practised on a very large scale in Lower Subansiri district.

- The *banana plantations, animal husbandry, poultry farming, etc., should be considered near ponds and tanks.* In this way the product of piggery, poultry, cow, etc., may be utilised for manure of the water of the ponds and tanks. This will provide basic nutrients to water, which also helps in maintaining the food chain of the fish. It will also reduce the expenditure for manure, supplementary feed and supervision, watch, etc.
- It was also observed that there is ample scope for improvement of fish production through appropriate input allocation. However, the parameters like producer's share in consumer's rupee as well as quantum of costs and margin indicate that existing system of fish marketing in the study area was by and large inefficient. *Hence, in order to enhance producer's share and to reduce the role of middleman, it is suggested to encourage the formation of fish farmer's co-operatives.*
- The fisheries may be included in the Agricultural Policy of the State Government or a separate policy for fishery is required in view of its immanence potential in the State.
- Finally, urgent attention is required from State Government to establish more Fish Farmers Development Agencies (FFDAs) in different parts of the State and make them more functional. The FFDAs should be more functional and committed to facilitate new techniques to the common fish farmers.

Thus, the study highlighted several vital issues relating to the opportunities and challenges of development of fisheries in Arunachal Pradesh. However, the fact is that the location specific attributes and dimensions of the fishery sector are too broad to be captured in a single framework. Hence, it is expected that the present study, i.e., productivity, resource use efficiency and marketing structure of inland fisheries of Arunachal Pradesh will form the basis of future research work of the region, in general and the State, in particular.

References

Arunachal Times (2012): *The Arunachal Times*, 14th September, 2012 Issue, Itanagar. (www.arunachaltimes.in)

Das, D. N. (2002): "Fish Farming in Rice Environments of North Eastern India", *Aquaculture Asia*, Vol. VII, No. 2, pp. 43-47.

Government of Arunachal Pradesh (2011): *Statistical Abstract of Arunachal Pradesh*, Directorate of Economics and Statistics, Itanagar.

Mahanta, P. C. *et al.* (2010): "Fishery Resources and Status of Fish Culture in Upland Waters of Arunachal Pradesh, India", in Mahanta, P. C. and D. Sarma (eds.), *Coldwater Fisheries Management*, Directorate of Coldwater Fisheries Research, Nainital, pp. 97-110.

Moda, T. (2005): "Status Paper on Fisheries of Arunachal Pradesh", in Tyagi, B. C. *et al.* (eds.), *Coldwater Fisheries Research and Development in North East Region of India*, National Research Centre on Coldwater Fisheries, Nainital, pp.139-144.

NEDFi (2007): *NEDFi Databank Quarterly*, Quarterly Journal on North Eastern States Economy Sericulture, Fisheries and Animal Husbandry, Vol. 5, I, II, III, and IV.

Appendix - I (A)

MAJOR FISH PRODUCING COUNTRIES OF WORLD, 2004

(in, '000 tonnes)

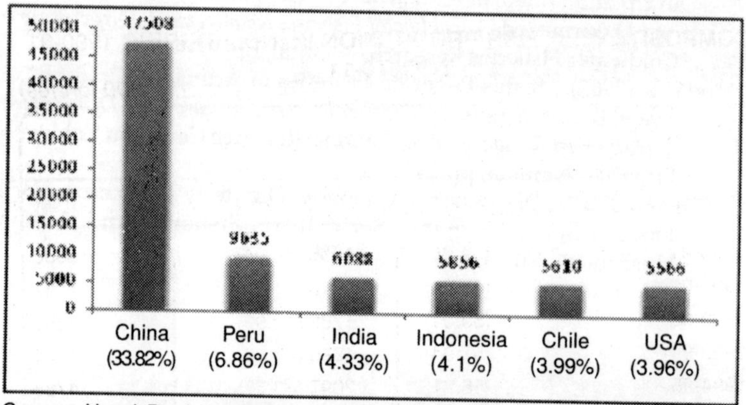

Source: Hand Book on Fisheries Statistics 2006, Department of Animal Husbandry, Dairying and Fisheries, Ministry of Agriculture, Government of India.

Appendix I (B)

MAJOR INLAND FISH PR ODUCING COUNTRIES OF WORLD, 2004

(in '000 tonnes)

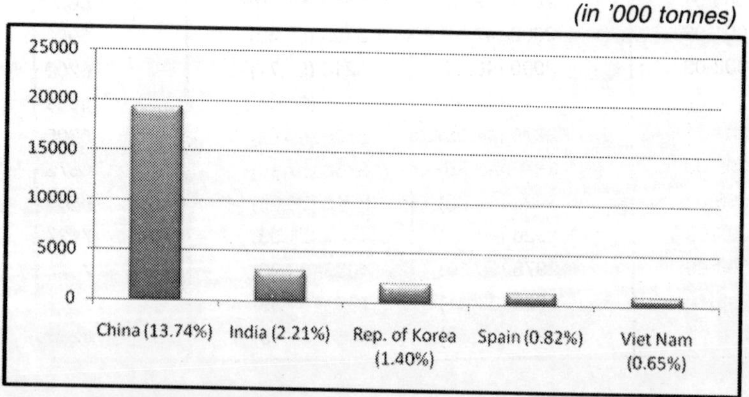

Source: Hand Book on Fisheries Statistics 2006, Department of Animal Husbandry, Dairying and Fisheries, Ministry of Agriculture, Government of India.

Appendix - II

COMPOSITION OF FISH PRODUCTION IN INDIA DURING 1990-91 TO 2010-11

(in, '000 tonnes)

Year	*Fish Production*		
	Marine	*Inland*	*Total*
1990-91	2300 (59.96)	1536 (40.04)	3836
1991-92	2447 (58.86)	1710 (41.14)	4157
1992-93	2576 (59.01)	1789 (40.99)	4365
1993-94	2649 (57.04)	1995 (42.96)	4644
1994-95	2692 (56.21)	2097 (43.79)	4789
1995-96	2707 (54.70)	2242 (45.30)	4949
1996-97	2967 (55.48)	2381 (44.52)	5348
1997-98	2950 (54.75)	2438 (45.25)	5388
1998-99	2696 (50.89)	2602 (49.11)	5298
1999-00	2852 (50.26)	2823 (49.74)	5675
2000-01	2811 (49.70)	2845 (50.30)	5656
2001-02	2830 (47.52)	3126 (52.48)	5956
2002-03	2990 (48.23)	3210 (51.77)	6200
2003-04	2941 (45.96)	3458 (54.04)	6399
2004-05	2779 (44.08)	3526 (55.92)	6305
2005-06	2816 (42.85)	3756 (57.15)	6572
2006-07	3024 (44.02)	3845 (55.98)	6869
2007-08	2920 (40.97)	4207 (59.03)	7127
2008-09	2978 (39.10)	4639 (60.90)	7617
2009-10	2689 (35.61)	4862 (64.39)	7551
2010-11	3220 (38.85)	5068 (61.15)	8288

Note: Figures in parentheses indicate the percentage to total.

Source: Annual Report 2011-12, Department of Animal Husbandry, Dairying and Fisheries, Ministry of Agriculture, New Delhi.

Appendix - III (A)

PER CAPITA CONSUMPTION OF FISH IN NORTH EASTERN REGION OF INDIA, 2009-10 *(in kg/person/month)*

State	*Per Capita Consumption (in kg)*		*Household Consumption of Fish (per 1000 household)*	
	Rural	*Urban*	*Rural*	*Urban*
Arunachal Pradesh	0.704	0.799	558	631
Assam	0.686	0.991	896	875
Manipur	0.342	0.509	692	906
Meghalaya	0.200	0.421	252	640
Mizoram	0.343	0.223	654	260
Nagaland	0.351	0.562	364	435
Sikkim	0.038	0.177	66	193
Tripura	1.177	1.488	976	938
INDIA	0.238	0.269	209	282

Source: Household Consumption of Various Goods and Services in India, NSS 66th Round (July 2009–June 2010), NSSO, Government of India, 2012.

Appendix - III (B)

PER CAPITA CONSUMPTION OF FISH IN ARUNACHAL PRADESH DURING 1993-94 TO 2009-10 *(in kg/person/month)*

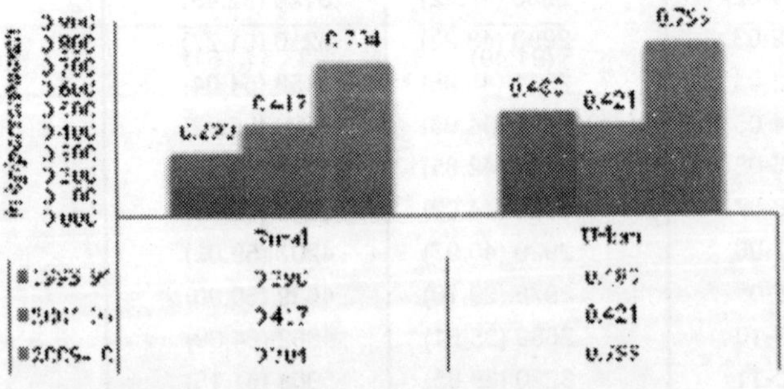

Sources: Household Consumption of Various Goods and Services in India, NSS 50th, 61st and 66th Round NSSO, Government of India.

Appendix - IV

COMPOSITION OF REVENUE AND CAPITAL EXPENDITURE IN FISHERY SECTOR BY CENTRAL GOVERNMENT DURING 1997-98 TO 2009-10

(in ₹ crore)

Year	*Expenditure in Fishery Department*		
	Revenue	*Capital*	*Total*
1997-98	32.01	4.16	36.17
1998-99	36.67	34.59	71.26
1999-00	38.56	13.62	52.18
2000-01	53.88	3.84	57.72
2001-02	61.82	2.27	64.09
2002-03	70.79	8.86	79.65
2003-04	51.31	8.91	60.22
2004-05	62.04	14.90	76.94
2005-06	81.44	1.69	83.13
2006-07	95.76	3.33	99.09
2007-08	119.19	1.01	120.20
2008-09	163.83	2.36	166.19
2009-10	247.65	4.21	251.86
Total	1114.95 (91.49)	103.75 (8.51)	1218.70

Note: Figures in parentheses indicate the percentage to total.

Source: http://indiabudget.nic.in/

Appendix - V

PRODUCTION AND REQUIREMENT OF FISH IN NORTH EASTERN STATES OF INDIA IN 2010-2011

States	*Production (in tonnes)*	*Requirement (in tonnes)*	*Deficit (in per cent)*
Arunachal Pradesh	3040	15269	80.09
Assam	227240	362771	37.36
Manipur	20200	33153	39.07
Meghalaya	4560	24837	81.64
Mizoram	2900	9844	70.54
Nagaland	6590	28878	77.18
Tripura	49230	56231	12.45
North Eastern Region (NER)	31760	57010	44.29

Sources: 1. NSSO, Government of India, 2012.

2. Annual Report 2011-12, Department of Animal Husbandry, Dairying and Fisheries, Ministry of Agriculture, New Delhi.

Appendix - VI

QUESTIONNAIRE

(Information being collected by this questionnaire is strictly confidential and will be used in the research purpose only)

1. Identification

1. Name of Household Head:
2. Age:
3. Sex: M/F
4. Category: (a) APST, (b) ST (from other States), (c) SC, (d) OBC, (e) General
5. Religion of the Household Head:
6. Name(s) of Respondent(s):
7. Village:
8. Circle:
9. Block:
10. Sub-Division:
11. District:
12. Pond: Owned/ Leased in/ Leased out/ Co-operative / Community owned.

2. Characteristics of Household Members

Use the following codes: Male-M, Female-F, Currently Married-CM, Never Married-NM, Widowed-W, Divorced-D, Separated-S, Literate-L and Illiterate-I:

Sl. No.	*Name*	*Relationship with HH Head*	*Age*	*Male/ Female*	*Marital Status*	*Years of Schooling*	*Literacy*
1.							
2.							
3.							
4.							
5.							
6.							
7.							
8.							
9.							
10							

3. Details of Working Members

Use the following codes: Male-M, Female-F Literate-L and Illiterate-I :

Sl. No.	Name	Sex	Age	Educational Level	Primary Occupation	Secondary Occupation
1.						
2.						
3.						
4.						
5.						
6.						

4. Land Owned by the Household Members

Specify the local units of land measures:

Type of Land	Total Area (in sq. metres)	Price	Value
1. Homestead			
2. Permanently cultivable Land			
3. Jhum Land			
4. Horticulture Land			
5. Forest			
6. Pond (Numbers:)			
7. River Area			
8. Others (specify)			

5. Crop Production in Last One Year

Sl. No.	Crops	Production	Consumption	Marketing
1	2	3	4	5
1.	Paddy			
2.	Maize			
3.	Millet			
4.	Mustard			
5.	Pulse			
6.	Potato			

(Contd.)

(*Contd.*)

1	2	3	4	5
7.	Palm			
8.	Ginger			
9.	Banana			
10.	Orange			
11.	Wild Spinach			
12.	Edible Leaf			
13.				
14.				

6. Size of the Water Area of the Ponds Tanks

Specify the local units of measures :

Types of the pond	*2009-10*	*2010-11*	*2011-12*
1. Owned pond 2. Leased out pond 3. Leased in pond 4. Operated water area 5. Current Unused or Fallow 6. Community owned pond			

7. Disposal of Fish Production

Channels of Disposal	*How disposed?*		
	2009-10	*2010-11*	*2011-12*
1. Wholly for personal consumption 2. Mainly personal consumption and partly marketing 3. Mainly marketing 4. Mainly marketing and partly personal consumption 5. Any other			

8. Material Inputs Cost *(in ₹/kg):*

Item	*2009-10*	*2010-11*	*2011-12*
1. Fish seeds			
2. Manures			
3. Fertilizers			
4. Pesticides			
5. Labour cost			
6. Fixed cost			
7. Rent			
8. Others (specify)			

9. Wholesale and Retail Prices *(in ₹/kg):*

Varieties of Fish	*2009-10*		*2010-11*		*2011-12*	
	Wholesale	*Retail*	*Wholesale*	*Retail*	*Wholesale*	*Retail*
1.						
2.						
3.						
4.						

10. Are you satisfied with price?

11. If not, what price do you expect?

12. What kind of constraints do you face in this case?

13. Income of Informants by various Sources over Years:

Sl. No.	*Sources*	*2009-10*	*2010-11*	*2011-12*
1	2	3	4	5
1.	Agriculture			
2.	Fishery			
3.	Horticultural crop			
4.	Forestry			

(Contd...)

1	2	3	4	5
5.	Arts and Crafts			
6.	Business			
7.	Transportation			
8.	Services			
9.	Agriculture Wages			
10.	Non-agriculture Wages			
11.	Any other services			

14. Package of Practices in Pisciculture

Items	*Whether used*	*Source*	*2009-10*		*2010-11*		*2011-12*	
			Quantity	*Value*	*Quantity*	*Value*	*Quantity*	*Value*
Seeds								
Manure								
Fertilizers								
Pesticides								
Fish meal								
Feeds								

15. Borrowings

Source of Borrowings	*Year*	*Amount*	*Rate of Interest*	*Purpose*	*Amount of Default*	*Reasons of Default*
1.						
2.						
3.						
4.						
5.						

16. Production Level during Previous Years

State the Production Level in Different Years (kg/acre)

Ponds/tanks	*2009-10*	*2010-11*	*2011-12*
1.			
2.			

17. If it is leased in pond then

1. Name of Pond Owner:
2. Age:
3. Sex: male/female
4. Category (Tick one):
   (a) APST
   (b) ST from other States
   (c) SC
   (d) OBC
   (e) General

18. In case of leased in pond, who bears the cost?

(a) Owner bears the entire cost
(b) Tenants bears the entire cost
(c) 50 : 50 sharing takes place
(d) Any other sharing agreements (specify)

18.1 What are the terms and conditions of leasing out of the ponds by the owner?

____

18.2 How the produce is shared between owner and leased-in fisherman?

____

19. Various Problems regarding Adoption of Modern Cultural Practices

Various Problems	*Whether faced or not by informant*	*Ranking of Problem*
1	2	3
1. Problem of lack of knowledge		
2. Non-planning		
3. Erratic supply of seeds and inadequate availability		

(*Contd.*)

(Contd...)

1	2	3
4. Problem of marketing		
5. Maintenance of ponds		
6. Problem of netting		
7. Problem of catching		
8. Problem of distance (location)		
9. Problem of finance		
10. Problem of ownership		
11. Risk factor and failure of extension services		
12. Lack of technical knowledge, training and supervision		
13. Problems of poaching		
14. Problems of mortality		
15. Problems of stealing		

20. Do you receive any Grant/Loan from Government Department/Agencies?

Yes/No

20.1 If Yes, Give Details (any other details please specify)

Year	*Name of Agency*	*Name of Programme*	*Amount*	*Amount pending*
2009-10				
2010-11				
2011-12				

Additional Questions:

- ✓ Between Agriculture and Pisciculture to which do you accord greater priority and why? Give reasons for your choice. ________________
- ✓ Is distance of location of water area a constraint? Yes/No
- ✓ If yes, why? ________________________
- ✓ Is the pond owned by you and cultivated by you? Yes/No

- ✓ Do you consider absentee ownership a constraint? Yes/No
- ✓ If yes, how? ____________________
- ✓ In case of multi-ownership, how many shareholders are there? ____________________
- ✓ How did you get water unit (Pond or tank): Inherit/Acquired through price given by you? ____________________
- ✓ Do you wholly own the water unit (pond or tank)? Yes/No
- ✓ If not, what is your share? ____________________
- ✓ Do you consider multiple ownerships a constraint? Yes/No
- ✓ If yes, state the ways in which it acts as a deterrent ____________________
- ✓ How do you consider a leased in pond less productive/more productive/equal productive in comparison to owned pond? ____________________
- ✓ State production per acre in your pond: ____________________
- ✓ Do you use modern varieties of fish seed? Yes/No
- ✓ If yes, according to schedule or according to resource availability? ____________________
- ✓ If not, what factors do you consider important (arrange according to priority) in not using varieties of seeds? High Price/Non-availability/Lack of interest/Lack of knowledge____________________
- ✓ Do you sell your produce in the market? Yes/No
- ✓ If yes, what is the channel? ____________________
- ✓ Do you consider the price you receive appropriate? Yes/No
- ✓ Do you have any idea about the final consumer's price? Yes/No

- ✓ What suggestion do you like to make in order to improve market efficiency? ____________________
- ✓ Are you aware about the services available with regard to technical knowledge about Pisciculture? Yes/No
- ✓ Do you face any problem regarding the shortage of water? Yes/No
- ✓ If yes, what types of problem? ____________________
- ✓ What are the major problems for you in scientific (composite) fish farming? ____________________
- ✓ What factors deter you from adopting scientific (composite) fish farming? ____________________
- ✓ Are you aware of the recommended schedule of stocking of fish seed? What is your source of collection of fish seed? ____________________
- ✓ Do you recognize the length of duration of lease term as factor for adopting intensive fish cultivation? Yes/No
- ✓ If yes, how are you benefited out of it? ____________________
- ✓ Do you get any assistance from FFDA schemes? ____________________
- ✓ Do you consider finance as a constraint? Yes/No
- ✓ In case of financial difficulties, how do you solve problems? ____________________
- ✓ Do you consider poaching/stealing a constraint? Yes/No
- ✓ If yes, what suggestion do you like to make in this regard? ____________________
- ✓ What is the approximate distance between pond/tank and the nearest market? ____________________
- ✓ What is the mode of transportation? ____________________

✓ Do you encounter any problem like fish diseases?

___

✓ If yes, what preventive measures do you normally adopt?

___

✓ From where you get medicine for fish diseases?

___

✓ Does Government organization provides enough helps? Yes/No

✓ What kinds of suggestions do you like to make to improve the working of the FFDA and other Government Programmes?

___

ANY OTHER OBSERVATIONS (SPECIFY) :

➢ ___

Signature of the Investigator:

Date:

Bibliography

Acharya, S. K. *et al.* (2009): *Livelihood, Income and Productivity in Fishery: The Synergy and Choice*, Agrotech Publishing Academy, Udaipur.

Agarwal, S. C. (2006): *History of Indian Fishery*, Daya Publishing House, Delhi.

Agbebi, F. O. (2010): "Salient Issues in Fish Marketing System in Nigeria", *Journal of Environmental Issues and Agriculture in Developing Countries*, Vol. 2, No. 1, pp. 94-105.

Ahmed, N. *et al.* (2009): "The Sustainable Livelihoods Approach to the Development of Freshwater Prawn Marketing Systems in Southwest Bangladesh", *Aquaculture Economics and Management*, Vol. 13, No. 3, pp. 246-269.

Alam, J. Md. *et al.* (2010): "A Study on Fish Marketing System in Swarighat, Dhaka, Bangladesh", *Nature and Science*, Vol. 8, No. 12, pp. 96-103.

Ali, A. B. (1990): "Rice/Fish Farming in Malaysia: A Resource Optimization", *Ambio*, Vol. 19, No. 8, pp. 404-408.

Allison, E. H. *et al.* (2007): "Enhancing the Resilience of Inland Fisheries and Aquaculture Systems to Climate Change", *SAT e Journal*, Vol. 4, Is. 1.

Andrew, P. (1999): *Economics of Brackishwater Shrimp Culture*, Daya Publishing House, Delhi.

Anene, A. *et al.* (2010): "Resources Use and Efficiency of Artisanal Fishing in Oguta, Imo State, Nigeria", *Journal of Development and Agricultural Economics*, Vol. 2, No. 3, pp. 094-099.

Anticamara, J.A. (2011): "Global fishing effort (1950–2010): Trends, gaps, and implications, *Fisheries Research*", Vol. 107, pp. 131-136.

Arnason, R. (1998): "Ecological Fisheries Management using Individual Transferable Share Quotas", *Ecological Fisheries Management*, Vol. 8, No. 1, pp. S151–S159.

Asamoah, E. K. (2012): "A Production Function Analysis of Pond Aquaculture in Southern Ghana", *Aquaculture Economics and Management*, Vol. 16, No. 3, pp. 183-201.

Awasti, M. And D. N. Das (2005): "Rice Field Fishery: An Asylum for Common Carp (Cyprinus Carpiol)", *Rajiv Gandhi University Research Journal*, Vol. 8, No. 2, pp. 26-33.

Ayyappan, S. and M. Krishna (2004), "Fisheries Sector in India: Dimensions of Development", *Indian Journal of Agricultural Economics*, Volume 59, No. 3, pp. 392-411.

Ayyappan, S. *et al.* (2006): *Handbook of Fisheries and Aquaculture*, Indian Council of Agricultural Research, New Delhi.

Barik, N. K. and P. K. Katiha (2003): "Management of Fisheries of Floodplain Wetlands: Institutional Issues and Options for Assam", in Kumar, A. *et al.* (eds.), *A Profile of People, Technologies and Policies in Fisheries Sector in India*, Workshop Proceedings Series 10, National Centre for Agricultural Economics and Policy Research, New Delhi, pp. 141-157.

Barua, P. *et al.* (2012): Fishing Industry andFisherfolk Existence through Micro-Credit Services for India and Bangladesh, *Bangladesh Research Publications Journal*, Vol. 7, No. 1, pp. 36-45.

Baruah, D. and K. Chisi (2009): "Fish Farming Practices in the High Altitudes of Arunachal Pradesh", *Arunachal Review*, Vol. XI, No. 5, pp. 6-9.

Bimbao, G. B. *et al.* (2000): "Socio-economics and production efficiency of tilapia hatchery operations in the Philippines", *Aquaculture Economics and Management*, Vol. 4, No. 1, pp. 47-61.

Bjørndal, T. (1987): "Production Economics and Optimal Stock Size in a North Atlantic Fishery", *The Scandinavian Journal of Economics*, Vol. 89, No. 2, pp. 145-164.

Bush, S. R. and S. Kosy (2007): "Geographical Distribution of Investment in Small-Scale Rural Fish Ponds", *Aquaculture Economics and Management*, Vol. 11, No. 3, pp. 285-311.

Carvalho, S. (2009): "Benthic dynamics within a land-based semi-intensive aquaculture fish farm: The importance of settlement ponds", *Aquacult Int*, Vol. 17, pp. 571-587.

Chakraborty, G. (2007): *An Economic Analysis of the Development of the Char Areas of Assam with Special Reference to Barpeta District*, (Ph.D. Thesis submitted to the Department of Economics, Dibrugarh University, Assam)

Choudhary *et al.* (2008): *Indigenous Knowledge and Policy Issues in Fisheries*, National Bureau of Fish Genetic Resources, ICAR, Lucknow.

Das, D. N. (2002): "Fish Farming in Rice Environments of North Eastern India", *Aquaculture Asia*, Vol. VII, No. 2, pp. 43-47.

Das, D. N. (2005): "Utilisation of Fishery Resources in Arunachal Pradesh, India: An Overview of Socio-economic Dimension", in Tyagi, B. C. *et al.* (eds.), *Coldwater Fisheries Research and Development in North East Region of India*, National Research Centre on Coldwater Fisheries, Nainital, pp. 25-36.

Das, D. N. *et al.* (2010): "Scope for mountain fishery based eco-tourism in Arunachal Pradesh: Potential and recommendations", in Mahanta, P. C. and D. Sarma (eds.), *Coldwater Fisheries Management*, Directorate of Coldwater Fisheries Research, Nainital, pp. 285-296.

Datta, S. K. and R. Kundu (2007): "Socio-Economic Appraisal of Culture Based Fishermen: Case Study in West Bengal", *Journal of Social Sciences*, Vol. 15, No. 3, pp. 255-262.

Debnath, B. *et al.* (2009): "Resource Use Efficiency and Social Profitability of an Integrated Aqua-Farm, Tripura, India", *Aquaculture Economics and Management*, Vol. 13, No. 4, pp. 344-354.

Dey, M. M. (2000): "Analysis of demand for fish in Bangladesh", *Aquaculture Economics and Management*, Vol. 4, No. 1, pp. 63-81.

Dey, M. M. (2005): "Disaggregated Analysis of Fish Supply, Demand, and Trade in Asia: Baseline Model and Estimation Strategy", *Aquaculture Economics and Management*, Vol. 9, No. 1, pp. 113-139.

Dey, M. M. (2005): "Fish Consumption and Food Security: A Disaggregated Analysis by Types of Fish and Classes of Consumers in Selected Asian Countries", *Aquaculture Economics and Management*, Vol. 9, No. 1, pp. 89-111.

Dey, M. M. (2005): "Technical Efficiency of Freshwater Pond Polyculture Production in Selected Asian Countries: Estimation and Implication", *Aquaculture Economics and Management*, Vol. 9, No. 1, pp. 39-63.

Dey, M. M. and A. Mahfuzuddin (2005): "Aquaculture-Food and Livelihoods for the Poor in Asia: A Brief Overview of the Issues", *Aquaculture Economics and Management*, Vol. 9, No. 1, pp.1-10.

Dey, M. M. *et al.* (2000): "Technical Efficiency of Tilapia Growout Pond Operations in the Philippines", *Aquaculture Economics and Management*, Vol. 4, No. 1, pp. 33-47.

Dey, M. M. *et al.* (2005): "Status and Economics of Freshwater Aquaculture in Selected Countries of Asia", *Aquaculture Economics and Management*, Vol. 9, No. 1, pp. 11-37.

Dupont, D. P. (1991): "Testing for Input Substitution in a Regulated Fishery", American *Journal of Agricultural Economics*, Vol. 73, No. 1, pp. 155-164.

Einspruch, E. L. (2005): *An Introductory Guide to SPSS for Windows*, 2nd ed., Sage Publications, New Delhi.

Ekpo, A. H. and L. E. Etim (1989): "The Performance of Nigeria's Fishery Sector: An Empirical Analysis, 1976-85", *Geo Journal*, Vol. 18, No. 3, pp. 291-295

Ellis, F. (1993): *Peasant Economics: Farm Households and Agrarian Development*, 2nd ed., Cambridge University Press, Great Britain.

Emokaro, C. O. and P. A. Ekunwe (2009): "Efficiency of resource-use and elasticity of production among catfish farmers in Kaduna, Nigeria", *African Journal of Biotechnology*, Vol. 8, No. 25, pp. 7249-7252.

FAO (2006): *The State of World Fisheries and Aquaculture*, FAO, UN, Rome.

FAO (2005): *FAO Training Series 24: Handbook on Small-Scale Freshwater Fish Farming*, Daya Publishing House, Delhi.

FAO (2010): *The State of World Fisheries and Aquaculture*, FAO, UN Rome.

FAO (2012): *The State of World Fisheries and Aquaculture*, FAO, UN, Rome.

Farrell, M.J. (1957) "The Measurement of Productive Efficiency," *Journal of the Royal Statistical Society*, vol. 120, pp. 253–281.

Gallet, C. A. (2009): The Demand for Fish: "A Meta-Analysis of the Own-Price Elasticity", *Aquaculture Economics and Management*, Vol. 13, No. 3, pp. 235-245.

Gaonkar, R. R. *et al.* (2006): *Fishes and Fisheries: Conservation and Sustainable Development*, APH Publishing Corporation, New Delhi.

Gaonkar, R. R. *et al.* (2008): *Fishery Management*, APH Publishing House, New Delhi.

Garcia, Y. *et al.* (2005): "Demand for Fish in the Philippines: A Disaggregated Analysis", *Aquaculture Economics and Management*, Vol. 9, No. 1, pp. 141-168.

Gaur, A. S. and S. S. Gaur (2011): *Statistical Methods for Practice and Research: A Guide to Data Analysis using SPSS*, 2nd ed., Response (A division of Sage Publication India Private Limited), New Delhi.

Ghosh, B. N. (2008): *Scientific Method and Social Research*, 3rd ed., Sterling Publishers Private Limited, New Delhi.

Goswami, M. *et al.* (2002): "Market Flow, Price Structure and Fish Marketing System in Assam—A Case Study", in *Proceedings of National Conference on Fisheries Economics, Extension and Management*, CIFE, Mumbai.

Government of Arunachal Pradesh. (1998): *Estimates of State Domestic Product of Arunachal Pradesh 1998*, Directorate of Economics and Statistics, Itanagar.

Government of Arunachal Pradesh (2002): *Tenth Five Year Plan* (2002-2007) and *Annual Plan* (2002-2003), Department of Planning, Itanagar.

Government of Arunachal Pradesh (2004): *Estimates of State Domestic Product of Arunachal Pradesh 2004*, Directorate of Economics and Statistics, Itanagar.

Government of Arunachal Pradesh (2005): *Arunachal Pradesh Human Development Report 2005*, Department of Planning, Itanagar.

Government of Arunachal Pradesh (2006): *Estimates of State Domestic Product of Arunachal Pradesh 2006*, Directorate of Economics and Statistics, Itanagar.

Government of Arunachal Pradesh (2007): *Eleventh Five Year Plan (2007-2012) and Annual Plan (2007-2008)*, Department of Planning, Itanagar.

Government of Arunachal Pradesh (2008): *Arunachal Pradesh District Gazetteers: Lohit District*, Directorate of Information and Public Relation, Itanagar.

Government of Arunachal Pradesh (2008): *Arunachal Pradesh District Gazetteers: Subansiri District*, Directorate of Information and Public Relation, Itanagar.

Government of Arunachal Pradesh (2011): *Statistical Abstract of Arunachal Pradesh*, Directorate of Economics and Statistics, Itanagar.

Government of Arunachal Pradesh (different Issues): *Annual Financial Statement of Arunachal Pradesh (different Issues)*, Department of Finance, Itanagar.

Government of India (1996): *Household Consumption of Various Goods and Services in India, 1993-94 NSS 50th Round (July 1993-June 1994)*, National Sample Survey Organisation, Ministry of Statistics and Programme Implementation, New Delhi.

Government of India (2001): *Report of the Working Group on Development and Management of Fisheries and Aquaculture for the Tenth Five Year Plan*, Planning Commission, New Delhi.

Government of India (2006): *Basic Statistics of North Eastern Region 2006*, North Eastern Council, Shillong.

Government of India (2006): *Report of the Working Group on Development and Management of Fisheries and Aquaculture for the Eleventh Five Year Plan*, Planning Commission, New Delhi.

Government of India (2007): *Handbook on Fisheries in India 2006*, Department of Animal Husbandry, Dairying and Fisheries, Ministry of Agriculture, New Delhi.

Government of India (2007): *Household Consumption of Various Goods and Services in India, 2004-05 NSS 61st Round (July 2004 - June 2005) Vol. I: Major States and All-India*, National Sample Survey Organisation, Ministry of Statistics and Programme Implementation, New Delhi.

Government of India (2009): *Arunachal Pradesh Development Report*, Planning Commission, New Delhi.

Government of India (2011): *Provisional Population Totals: Paper 2, Vol. 1 of 2011 Rural-Urban Distribution of Arunachal Pradesh Series 13*, Census of India 2011.

Government of India (2011): *Annual Report 2010-11*, Department of Animal Husbandry, Dairying and Fisheries, Ministry of Agriculture, New Delhi.

Government of India (2011): *Report of the Working Group on Development and Management of Fisheries and Aquaculture for the XII Five Year Plan: 2012-17*, Planning Commission, New Delhi.

Government of India (2012): *Annual Report 2011-12*, Department of Animal Husbandry, Dairying and Fisheries, Ministry of Agriculture, New Delhi.

Government of India (2012): *Household Consumption of Various Goods and Services in India, 2004-05 NSS 66th Round (July 2009 - June 2010)*, National Sample Survey Organisation, Ministry of Statistics and Programme Implementation, New Delhi.

Gujarati, D. N. (2005): *Basic Econometrics*, 4th ed., Tata McGraw-Hill Publishing Company Limited, New Delhi.

Gurung, T. B. et al. (2005): "Participatory Fisheries Management for Livelihood Improvement of Fishers in Phewa Lake, Pokhara, Nepal", *Himalayan Journal of Sciences*, Vol. 3, Is. 5, pp. 47-52.

Hall, C. B. (2002): *Ponds and Fish Culture*, Agrobios (India), Jodhpur.

Hatch, U. and C. F. Tai (1997): "A Survey of Aquaculture Production Economics and Management", *Aquaculture Economics and Management*, Vol. 1, No. 1, pp. 13-27.

Hays, W. L. (1981): *Statistics*, 3rd ed., CBS College Publishing, Holt.

Henderson, J. M. and R. E. Quandt (2010): *Microeconomic Theory: A Mathematical Approach*, 3rd ed., Tata McGraw Hill Education Private Limited, New Delhi.

Inoni, O.E. (2007): "Allocative Efficiency in Pond Fish Production in Delta State, Nigeria: A Production Function Approach", *Agricultura Tropica ET Subtropica* Vol. 40, No. 4, pp. 127-134.

Jagger, P. and J. Pender (2001): "Markets, Marketing and Production Issues for Aquaculture in East Africa: The Case of Uganda", *Naga*, Vol. 24, Nos. 1 & 2, pp. 42-51.

Jana, B. B. and C. D. Webster (eds.) (2005): *Sustainable Aquaculture: Global Perspectives*, Atlantic Publishers and Distributors, Delhi.

Johnston, J. (1972): *Econometric Method*, 2nd ed., McGraw-Hill Kogakusha, Ltd., Tokyo, Japan.

Joshua U.A *et al.* (2012): "Economic Viability of Cat Fish Farming in Nasarawa State", *Production Agriculture and Technology*, Vol. 8, No. 1, pp. 144-152.

Katiha, P. K. *et al.* (2005): "Inland Aquaculture in India: Past Trend, Present Status and Future Prospects", *Aquaculture Economics and Management*, Vol. 9, No. 1, pp. 237-264.

Khanna, D. R. and S. Singh (2002): *Pond Fish Ecology and Economics*, Daya Publishing House, Delhi.

Korakandy, R. (1996): *Economics of Fisheries Management: A Critique in Third World Perspective*, Daya Publishing House, Delhi.

Koutsoyiannis, A. (1979): *Modern Microeconomics*, 2nd ed., Macmillan Press Ltd., Hong Kong.

Koutsoyiannis, A. (2004): *Theory of Econometrics*, 2nd ed. Palgrave, New Delhi.

Kumar, A. (2004):"Export Performance of Indian Fisheries: Strengths and Challenges Ahead", *Economic and Political Weekly*, Vol. 39, No. 38, pp. 4264-4270.

Kumar, A. *et al.* (eds.) (2003): *A Profile of People, Technologies and Policies in Fisheries Sector in India*, Workshop Proceedings Series 10, National Centre for Agricultural Economics and Policy Research, New Delhi.

Kumar, B. G. *et al.* (2008): "Domestic Fish Marketing in India-Changing Structure, Conduct, Performance and Policies", *Agricultural Economics Research Review*, Vol. 21 (Conference Number), pp. 345-354.

Kumar, B. G. *et al.* (2010): "Marketing System and Efficiency of Indian Major Carps in India", *Agricultural Economics Research Review*, Vol. 23, pp. 105-113.

Kumar, H. D. (2003): *Sustainability and Management of Aquaculture and Fisheries*, Daya Publishing House, Delhi.

Kumar, P. and M. M. Dey (2004): "A Study of Modelling of Household Demand for Fisheries in India", *Indian Journal of Agricultural Economics*, Vol. 59, No.3, pp. 465-475.

Kumar, P. *et al.* (2005): "Demand for Fish by Species in India: Three-stage Budgeting Framework", *Agricultural Economics Research Review*, Vol. 18, pp. 167-186.

Kumar, P. *et al.* (2006): "Fish Supply Projections by Production Environments and Species Types in India", *Agricultural Economics Research Review*, Vol. 19, pp. 327-351.

Kurien, J. (1985): "Technical Assistance Projects and Socio-Economic Change: Norwegian Intervention in Kerala's Fisheries Development", *Economic and Political Weekly*, Vol. 20, No. 25/26, pp. A70-A88.

Lee, J. M. *et al.* (2006): "Demand for Aquaculture Products in Taiwan: An Application of the Generalized Model", *Aquaculture Economics and Management*, Vol. 10, No. 1, pp. 47-57.

Li, L. and J. Huang (2005): "China's Accession to the WTO and Its Implications for the Fishery and Aquaculture Sector", *Aquaculture Economics and Management*, Vol. 9, No. 1, pp. 195-215.

Loc, V. T. T. *et al.* (2010): "High and low value fish chains in the Mekong Delta: Challenges for Livelihoods and Governance", *Environment Development and Sustainability*, Vol. 12, pp. 889-908.

Maddala, G. S. (2009): *Introduction to Econometrics*, 3rd ed., Willey India Pvt. Ltd., New Delhi.

Madugu, A.J. and A. Edward (2011): "Marketing and Distribution Channel of Processed Fish in Adamawa State, Nigeria", *Global Journal of Management and Business Research*, Vol. 11, No. 4, Ver. 1.0.

Mahanta, P. C. and D. Sarma (ed.) (2010): *Coldwater Fisheries Management*, Directorate of Coldwater Fisheries Research, Nainital.

Mahanta, P. C. *et al.* (2010): "Fishery Resources and Status of Fish Culture in Upland Waters of Arunachal Pradesh, India", in Mahanta, P. C. and D. Sarma (eds.), *Coldwater Fisheries Management*, Directorate of Coldwater Fisheries Research, Nainital, pp. 97-110.

Mandal, S. *et al.* (2007): "Agribusiness Opportunities of Ornamental Fisheries in North-Eastern Region of India", *Agricultural Economics Research Review*, Vol. 20 (Conference Issue), pp. 471-488.

Mason, R. D. (1978): *Statistical Techniques in Business and Economics*, 4th ed., Richard D. Irwin, Inc. Homewood, Illinois.

Meehean, O.L. (1952): "Problems of Farm Fish Pond Management", *The Journal of Wildlife Management*, Vol. 16, No. 3, pp. 233-238.

Misra J. (2009): *Problems and Prospects of Inland Aquaculture in West Bengal – A Case Study*, (Ph.D. Thesis).

Misra, S. R. (1987): *Fisheries in India*, Ashis Publishing House, New Delhi.

Misra, S. R. (2006): *Inland Fisheries in India: Issues and Concerns*, Concept Publishing Company, New Delhi.

Misra, S. R. (2012): *Sustainable Rural Livelihood Systems: The Case for India's Inland Fisheries Sector*, Concept Publishing Company (P) Ltd., New Delhi.

Mitra, A. (1997): *Internal Migration and Economic Development in the Hills*, Omsons Publication, New Delhi.

Mitra, A. (1998): "Environment and Sustainable Development in Hilly Regions of North East India — A Study of Arunachal Pradesh", *International Journal of Social Economics*, Vol.25, No. 24, pp. 196-206.

Mitra, A. (2000): "Regional Disparities in Economic development: An Inter-district Empirical Study of Arunachal Pradesh", *Journal of North-East India Council for Social Science Research*, Vol. 24, No.1, pp. 46-55.

Mitra, A. (2005): "Transformation of Arunachal's Economy: Opportunities and Challenges for a Less Developed State", *Indian Development Review*, Vol. 4, No. 2, pp. 433-440.

Mitra, A. and K. Nath (2013): "Challenges and Issues of

Development in Border Areas-A Study of Eastern—most Border State of India", *Northeast Researches*, Vol. IV, No. 4, pp. 99-117.

Mitra, A. and K. Nath (2013): "Opportunities and Socio-economic Issues in Inland Fisheries Development of North Eastern Region of India: An Empirical Study of Arunachal Pradesh", *Arthshodh*, Vol. III, No. 1 (in press).

Moda, T. (2005): "Status Paper on Fisheries of Arunachal Pradesh", in Tyagi, B. C. et al. (eds.), *Coldwater Fisheries Research and Development in North East Region of India*, National Research Centre on Coldwater Fisheries, Nainital, pp.139-144.

Nakamura, R. (1958): "Aquaculture Development in India: A Model", *Bioscience*, Vol. 35, No. 2, pp. 96-100.

Nam, S. and B. Roitana (2005): "A Review of Inland Fisheries Management in Cambodia", *Asian Productivity Organization (APO) and the International Seminar on Inland Fisheries Management*, 21-26 September 2005, New Delhi, India.

Nath, D. (1996): "Significance of Fisheries in the Life of Apatani Tribe", *Arunachal University Research Journal*, Vol. 1, pp. 86-97.

Nath, K. *et al.* (2013): "Prospects of Microfinance in Fishery Sector of Arunachal Pradesh" in Sarmah, G. N. (eds.), *Microfinance and Sustainable Development in North East India*, Commonwealth Publishers Pvt. Ltd. New Delhi, pp. 241-249.

Nath, P. and S.C. Dey (2000), *Fish and Fisheries of North Eastern India, Volume-I, Arunachal Pradesh*, Narendra Publishers, New Delhi.

NEDFi (2007): *NEDFi Databank Quarterly*, Quarterly Journal on North Eastern States Economy Sericulture, Fisheries and Animal Husbandry, Vol. 5, Iss. II, III, and IV.

Ogundari, K. and S. O. Ojo (2009): "An Examination of Income Generation Potential of Aquaculture Farms in Alleviating Household Poverty: Estimation and Policy Implications from Nigeria", *Turkish Journal of Fisheries and Aquatic Sciences*, Vol. 9, pp. 39-45.

Olagunju, F. I. *et al.* (2007): "Economic Viability of Cat Fish Production in Oyo State, Nigeria", *Journal of Human Ecology*, Vol. 21, No. 2, pp. 121-124.

Oliver, P. (2008): *Writing Your Thesis*, 2nd ed., Sage Publication India Private Limited, New Delhi.

Olubunmi, A. and A. F. Bankole (2012): "Determinants of Income from Fish Marketing in Ibarapa Area of Oyo State, Nigeria", *Science Journal of Agricultural Research and Management*, Vol. 2012, Article ID sjarm-135, p. 6.

Oo, W. (2002): "Inland Fisheries of the Union of Myanmar", in Petr, T. and Swar, D.B. (eds.) *Cold Water Fisheries in the Trans-Himalayan Countries*, FAO Fisheries Technical Paper, No. 431, FAO, Rome, pp. 70-76.

Pandey, P. N. et al. (2005): *Economics of Fisheries*, APH Publishing Corporation, New Delhi.

Patil, A. (2012): "Economic Valuation of Reservoirs in Terms of Agricultural Productivity and Fishery in Dry Region of Sangli District, Maharashtra", *Biological Forum—An International Journal*, Vol. 4, No. 21, pp. 10-14.

Petr, T. and Swar, D.B. (eds.) (2002): *Cold Water Fisheries in the Trans-Himalayan Countries*, FAO Fisheries Technical Paper, No. 431, FAO, Rome.

Petr, M. And G. Rugg (2010): *The Unwritten Rules of PhD Research*, Tata McGraw Hill Education Private Limited, New Delhi.

Phillips, M. J. *et al.* (2002): "Environment, Livelihoods and Indigenous Cold Water Fishes" in Petr, T. and Swar, D.B. (eds.) *Cold Water Fisheries in the Trans-Himalayan Countries*, FAO Fisheries Technical Paper, No. 431, FAO, Rome, pp. 39-46.

Phyne, P. (2010): "A Comparative Political Economy of Rural Capitalism: Salmon Aquaculture in Norway, Chile and Ireland", *Acta Sociologica*, Vol. 53, No. 2, pp. 160–180.

Prasad, J. and A. Prasad (ed.) (1995): *Indian Agricultural Marketing: Emerging Trends and Perspectives*, Mittal Publications, New Delhi.

Pushpalatha, K. B. C. and J. Chandrasoma (2010): "Culture-Based Fisheries in Minor Perennial Reservoirs in Sri Lanka: Variability in Production, Stocked Species and Yield Implications", *Journal Applied Ichthyology*, Vol. 26, pp. 99-104

Raimiyar, G. P. (1998): "Adoption of management and

technological practices by fishpond operators in Nepal", *Aquaculture Economics and Management*, Vol. 2, No. 3, pp. 89- 99.

Rao, A. S. and D. Tyagi (2009): *Research Methodology with SPSS*, Shree Niwas Publications, Jaipur.

Ray, S. (ed.) (2011): *Handbook of Agriculture in India*, Oxford University Press, New Delhi.

Robards, M. D. and J. A. Greenberg (2007): "Global Constraints on Rural Fishing Communities: Whose Resilience is it Anyway?", *Fish and Fisheries* , Vol. 8, pp. 14-30.

Roy, T. N. (2008): "Analysis of Marketing of Fish Fingerlings and Environmental Awareness Level of Fishermen in Dakshin Dinajpur District of West Bengal", *Agricultural Economics Research Review*, Vol. 21 (Conference Number), pp. 425-432.

Saikia, S. K. and D. N. Das (2008): "Rice-Fish Culture and its Potential in Rural Development: A Lesson from Apatani Farmers, Arunachal Pradesh, India", *Journal of Agriculture and Rural Development*, Vol. 6, No. (1&2), pp. 125-131.

Schwindt, R. *et al.* (2000): "Net Loss: A Cost-Benefit Analysis of the Canadian Pacific Salmon Fishery", *Journal of Policy Analysis and Management*, Vol. 19, No. 1, pp. 23-45.

Sharma, K. R. (1999): "Technical Efficiency of Carp Production in Pakistan", *Aquaculture Economics and Management*, Vol. 3, No. 2, pp. 131-141.

Sharma, K. R. *et al.* (1998): "Technical Efficiency of Carp Production in Nepal: An Application of Stochastic Frontier Production Function Approach", *Aquaculture Economics and Management*, Vol. 2, No. 3, pp. 129-140.

Shepderd, G.S (1975). Farm Products-Economic Analysis. Iowa State University Press, Iowa, USA.

Shrestha, T.K. (2002): "Cold Water Fisheries Development in Nepal", in Petr, T. and Swar, D.B. (eds.) *Cold Water Fisheries in the Trans-Himalayan Countries*, FAO Fisheries Technical Paper, No. 431, FAO, Rome, pp. 47-58.

Simon R. and K. Sonsai (2007): "Geographical Distribution of Investment in Small-Scale Rural Fish Ponds", *Aquaculture Economics and Management*, Vol. 11, No. 3, pp. 285-311.

Singh, B. (2007): *Fishery Management—Planning and Objectives*, Vista International Publishing House, Delhi.

Singh, B.B. *et al.*(2000): "Production and Marketing of Inland Fish—A Case Study" in. J. Prasad and A. Prasad (eds.), *Indian Agricultural Marketing: Emerging Trends and Perspectives*, Mittal Publications, New Delhi, India, pp. 279-287.

Singh, K. M. *et al.* (2007): *Fishery Sector and Fish Workers in India: An Overview*, V. V. Giri National Labour Institute, Noida.

Singh, R. K. P. (2003): *Economics of Aquaculture*, Daya Publishing House, Delhi.

Swar, D. B. (2002): "The Status of Cold Water Fish and Fisheries in Nepal and Prospects of their Utilization for Poverty Reduction", in Petr, T. and Swar, D.B. (eds.) *Cold Water Fisheries in the Trans-Himalayan Countries*, FAO Fisheries Technical Paper, No. 431, FAO, Rome, pp. 77-94.

Tatung, T. (2000): *A Study of Dynamics of Agricultural Practices among the Apatanis of Arunachal Pradesh*, (M. Phil. Dissertation submitted to the Department of Tribal Studies, Rajiv Gandhi University, Itanagar).

Thomas, D. H. L. (1996): "Fisheries Tenure in an African Floodplain Village and the Implications for Management", *Human Ecology*, Vol. 24, No. 3, pp. 287-313.

Tyagi, B. C. *et al.* (eds.) (2005): *Coldwater Fisheries Research and Development in North East Region of India*, National Research Centre on Coldwater Fisheries, Nainital.

Umoh, G. S. (2006): "Resource Use Efficiency in Urban Farming: An Application of Stochastic Frontier Production Function", *International Journal of Agriculture and Biology*, Vol. 8, No. 1, pp. 38-44.

Vankhede, G. N. and S. V. Deshmukh (2002): *Freshwater Fishculture: Development and Management*, Sarup & Sons Publishers, New Delhi.

Viner, K. *et al.* (2006): "Development of Fisheries Co-management in Cambodia: A case study and its implications", *Discussion Series No. 2*, World Fish Center Contribution No. 1788, Malaysia.

World Bank (2004): Socio-cultural Aspects of Developing Small Scale Fisheries, Vol. 73.

Yaqoob, M. (2002): "Cold Water Fisheries of Pakistan", in Petr, T. and Swar, D.B. (eds.) *Cold Water Fisheries in the Trans-Himalayan Countries,* FAO Fisheries Technical Paper, No. 431, FAO, Rome, pp. 99-104.

Young, P. V. (2009): *Scientific Social Surveys and Research,* 6th ed., PHI Learning Private Limited, New Delhi.

Zaman, T. *et al.* (2006): "Present Status of Pond Fishery Resources and Livelihood of the Fish Farmers of Mohanpur Upazila in Rajshahi District", *University Journal of Zoology, Rajshahi University,* Vol. 25, pp. 31-35.

Zen, L.W. *et al.* (2002): "Technical Efficiency of the Driftnet and Payang Seine (Lampara) Fisheries in West Sumatra", Indonesia, *Asian Fisheries Science,* Vol. 15, pp. 97-106.

Zwirn, M. (2002): "Aquaculture in Egypt: Improving Food Security and Resolving Resource Allocation Conflicts", *Journal of Environment & Development,* Vol. 11, No. 2, pp. 129-148.

Website/ Webpage Accessed

http://arunachalipr.gov.in/

http://arunachalipr.gov.in/Dowmloads/State%20map.jpg

http://arunachalplan.gov.in/

http://arunachalpradesh.nic.in/

http://arunachalpradesh.nic.in/images/state_map.jpg

http://arunagri.com/climate.asp

http://db.nedfi.com/

http://db.nedfi.com/content/economy-arunachal-pradesh

http://db.nedfi.com/content/net-state-domestic-product-arunachal-pradesh

http://en.wikipedia.org/wiki/Lohit_district

http://en.wikipedia.org/wiki/Lower_Subansiri_district

http://online.sagepub.com/

http://www. arunachalpradesh.nic.in

http://www. ejournal.icrisat.org

http://www.arunachaltimes.in

http://www.banglajol.info/index.php/jard

http://www.dahd.nic.in/dahd/reports.aspx

http://www.dahd.nic.in/dahd/reports/annual-report-2004-05.aspx

http://www.dahd.nic.in/dahd/upload/AnnualReport2009-10.pdf

http://www.dahd.nic.in/dahd/WriteReadData/Arunachal%20Pradesh%202.pdf

http://www.dahd.nic.in/dahd/WriteReadData/Assam%202.pdf

http://www.dahd.nic.in/dahd/WriteReadData/Manipur%202.pdf

http://www.dahd.nic.in/dahd/WriteReadData/Meghalaya%202.pdf

http://www.dahd.nic.in/dahd/WriteReadData/Mizoram%202.pdf

http://www.dahd.nic.in/dahd/WriteReadData/Nagaland%202.pdf

http://www.dahd.nic.in/dahd/WriteReadData/Sikkim%202.pdf

http://www.dahd.nic.in/dahd/WriteReadData/Tripura%202.pdf

http://www.db.nedfi.com

http://www.fao..org

http://www.fao.org/docrep/005/y7300e/y7300e00.htm

http://www.fao.org/docrep/007/y5600e/y5600e00.htm

http://www.fao.org/docrep/009/A0699e/A0699e00.htm

http://www.fao.org/docrep/011/i0250e/i0250e00.htm

http://www.fao.org/docrep/013/i1820e/i1820e00.htm

http://www.fao.org/docrep/016/i2727e/i2727e00.htm

http://www.fao.org/docrep/016/i2727e/i2727e00.htm

http://www.fao.org/index_en.htm

http://www.icar.org.in

http://www.indiabudget.nic.in

http://www.jccc-ugcinfonet.in/

http://www.jstor.org/

http://www.mospi.nic.in

http://www.nabard.org

http://www.nedfi.net/

http://www.onefivenine.com/images/DistrictMaps/32.jpg

http://www.onefivenine.com/images/DistrictMaps/34.jpg

http://www.patnsukjournal.net/currentissue

http://www.rbi.org

http://www.thisismyindia.com/arunachal-pradesh/images/arunachal-pradesh.png

http://arunagri.com/resources/images/table/Physica_and_Chemical/PhysiChemiMap.png

Index

Administrative change, 60–61
Adulteration, 27, 99, 102–3, 128
Agriculture/Agricultural
  allied activities, 1, 38, 56
  commodities, 28
  growth rate, 38
  land, 4
  measurement of output, 11
  output, 11
  policy, 130
  production, 1
  trading, 2
Agro-climatic zones, 6–7, 59, 97, 122
Allied Activities, 56
Animal husbandry, 7, 39, 71, 73, 75, 120, 130, 133
Animal protein, 29
Apatani plateau, 3, 6, 50, 115
Aquaculture, 2, 14, 16–18, 22, 28–29, 31, 39–40, 65, 107, 110, 114, 117, 129
  department, 8, 19
  farms, 19
  global, 38
  modern, 15
  packages, 128
  practices, 14, 107
  production, 19
  technologies, 17
Aquatic organisms, 30
Aquatic resources, 21, 53, 97
Arunachal Pradesh Reorganization of Districts Act, 61
Asian food production system, 14

Balipara Frontier Tract, 63
Benefit Cost Ratio (BCR), 88, 125
Brackish water Fish Farmer Development Agency, 107
Brahmaputra river, 44

Capital expenditure, 105, 116, 135
Carp production, 16
Cash income, 2
Catfish
  farmers, 21
  production, 21
Cattle watering, 75
Centrally Sponsored Schemes, 107–8
Central sector schemes, 37, 107, 109, 117
Climate change, 22
Cobb-Douglas production function, 9, 16, 89, 125
Coefficient, 91, 126
  negative, 84, 123
  positive, 83, 86, 123–24
Cold water
  aquaculture, 107
  character, 17
  fish, 18
  fisheries, 17, 22, 55, 109, 116–17
  zone, 31
Commercial
  activity, 62
  market, 4
Commission agents, 30
Composite carp production system, 128

Cost-benefit analysis, 9, 12, 17, 86
Cost-effective practices, 31
Costs and margins, 92
Crop Production, 31, 138
Cultivable land area, 84–86, 124

Dairying, 7, 39, 133
Department of Animal Husbandry, 7, 39, 133
Derelict water, 3, 44, 50, 114–15
Derelict water bodies, 38
Discount method, 88
District paddy-cum-fish culture, 84
Districts Act, 61
District-wise Composition of Fish Production in Arunachal Pradesh, 56
Domestic marketing, 25
Duck-cum-fish culture, 129

Econometric analysis, 12, 122
Economic
  activities, 2, 31, 61
  growth, 37
  inputs, 20
Environmental
  change, 29
  factors, 21
Expense Structure Ratio (ESR), 88, 125
Exponential growth rate, 41–42, 54, 114

Farmer-herder-fishers, 22
Farming activities, 66
Feeding, 69, 119
Fingerlings, 19–21, 27, 69, 91, 126
Fish
  breed, 129
  budget, 29
  catching, 3
  consumption, 18, 27, 29
  crop, 30
  cultivation, 7
  -cum-duck culture, 74, 120
  dried, 31
  expensive, 29
  farms, 5, 106
  feed, 102–3
  fingerlings, 25
  fresh, 24, 31
  frozen, 26
  -income classes, 27
  indigenous, 28
  larvae, 20
  low-price, 29
  marketers, 26
  marketing efficiency of, 94, 127
  native, 20
  ornamental, 32
  price of, 91, 126
  selling, 2
Fishery/Fisheries
  cultural, 3
  driftnet, 20
  floodplain, 28
  global, 40
  lampara, 20
  marine, 40
  multi-gear, 20
  ornamental, 32
  small-scale, 23, 38
  sports, 128
  sustainable, 2, 40
  production, 18
  activities, 76
  practices, 3, 53, 96
  -related livelihood, 2
Fish farmers, 5, 7, 15–16, 23–24, 26, 66–67, 70–71, 85, 87–88, 96–97, 99–102, 107, 118–20, 123, 128–29
  age of, 86, 124
  co-operatives, 130
  education level of, 67, 118
  gender of, 86, 124
  illiterate, 118
  matured, 118
  occupational structure, 71
  poor, 17, 24
  private, 129
  small-scale, 38
Fish Farmers' Development Agencies (FFDAs), 107, 110–12, 117, 130

Fish farming, 4, 7, 9, 12, 14–15, 24, 66, 70, 86–88, 96–97, 102, 115, 118, 125, 128–29
  activities, 4, 69–70
  commercial, 97
  evaluation of Government policies, 96
  rice-based, 31
Fishing, 3, 20, 22–23, 38, 53, 61–62, 69–72, 85, 119, 123
  activities, 23, 67–68, 70, 119
  artisanal, 20
  direct, 3, 53
  driftnet, 20
  fulltime, 2
  pressure, 23
  traditional, 54
Fish markets, 18, 24–26, 31–32, 69, 92–93, 99, 127
  domestic, 25, 28
Fishpond owners, 93, 127
Fish production, 2, 20, 25, 27, 40, 44–45, 53–56, 70, 72, 79, 86–91, 114, 116, 118–19, 125–26
  marine, 1, 40–42
  ornamental, 32
Fish seeds, 77, 89–91, 102, 125–26
Fish species, 15, 29, 44–45, 114
Five Year Plan
  Second, 103
  Fourth, 103
  Sixth, 40
  Tenth, 107, 109, 117
  Eleventh, 107
Flash flood, 53, 97, 127
Flood plains, 38
Food and Agriculture Organisation, 8
Food
  insecurity, 37–38
  resources, 3, 53
  security, 37–38
  self-sufficiency, 37
Foreign exchange, 27
Forestry, 71, 73
Freshwater, 28
  aquaculture, 17, 107, 109, 117
  fish biodiversity, 44, 114
  fish culture, 110
  fisheries, 45, 115

Gender distribution, 68
Gender role, 69, 118
Government intervention, 53, 96, 116
Government legislation, 27
Government Policies, 13, 17, 96
Government Source, 121
Grassroots levels, 129
Gross Domestic Product (GDP), 42, 44, 114
Gross fish production, 10
Gross margin, 19, 79, 86–87, 91, 124–25

Hill districts, 6, 55, 57, 64, 78, 80–81, 116, 121–22, 128
Himalayan region, 22
Hindu Kush, 22
Horticulture, 71–75, 96, 120

Income elasticities, 27
Income poverty, 19
Indian Major Carps (IMC), 25
Individualization, 3–4
Industrial production, 14
Inefficient marketing structure, 97, 99, 101, 127–28
Information dissemination, 25
Infrastructural facilities, 9, 25, 81–82, 123
Inland
  fish cultivation, 14
  fish production, 2, 42, 44, 107, 114
  fisheries, 2, 4, 12, 14, 32, 38, 40, 114, 130
  fishery resources, 38
  resources, 2
  water fisheries, 3, 29, 50, 115
  water resources, 38–39, 44, 50
Input-related practices, 18

Kolleru Lake Area (KLA), 25

Lakes, 17, 23, 38, 44, 50–51, 54, 61, 106, 114–15, 128
 natural, 61
 plain, 3
Lakhimpur Frontier Tract, 63
Landing centres, 39
Large water area, 97
Leafy vegetables, 11
Livelihood
 assets, 24
 diversification, 2, 22
 enhancement, 1, 21–22
 insecurity, 37
 security, 26
 strategies, 12, 22
 Strategies, 73
Lohit Frontier Division, 60–61

Management
 objectives, 23, 30
 practices, 16–17
 -related practices, 18
Managerial efficiency, 86
Marginal
 farmers, 31
 productivity, 17
 value productivities, 10, 91, 94, 126
 value products, 90
Market
 availability, 32
 chain, 26
 demand, 45, 114
 intermediaries, 25
 performance, 93
 prices, 20, 24
 -related constraints, 32
 structure, 26
Marketing
 activities, 25, 69, 92, 119
 channels, 10, 25, 94
 cost, 93
 efficiency, 10–11, 25, 93–94, 127
 index of efficiency, 11
 management, 27
 margin, 92, 101, 127
 practices, 67
 structure, 4, 10, 12, 14–15, 24, 32 79, 91, 113, 126, 130
Material Inputs Cost, 140
Medium pond farming, 86, 124
Mishmi Hills, 61
Monetized transactions, 3
Multipurpose activity, 76, 121

Natural resources, 1, 15, 24
Net District Domestic Product (NDDP), 61, 64
Net return analysis, 86
Net State Domestic Product (NSDP), 46, 55
North Eastern Frontier Tract, 61, 63
North East Frontier Agency, 61
Nucleus activity, 110

Optimal levels, 20
Organic fertilization, 65
Ornamental fish production units, 32

Paddy-cum-fish culture, 6, 44, 50–51, 55, 64, 74, 81, 94, 96, 115, 120, 122, 129
Physico-chemical change, 20
Piggery-cum-fish culture, 129
Pond fishery resources, 23
Ponds and water bodies, 66, 77
Post-Harvest Infrastructure, 107, 109, 117
Poverty levels, 20
Prawn production, 18
Production
 economics, 16
 elasticities, 10, 90
 frontier, 16
 function analysis, 17, 89
 resources, 21
Productive resources, 19

Quantitative Analysis, 79

Rate of Return (RoR), 88, 125
Record-keeping-related practices, 18
Regional cooperation, 28
Regression
 analysis, 19, 82
 coefficient, 10

Resource
- allocation, 32, 72
- assets, 38
- boundaries, 23
- constraints, 11
- -use efficiency, 4, 12, 14–15, 19, 21, 26, 32, 79, 89, 91, 113, 130
- utilisation, 19

Resource Cost Ratio (RCR), 31
Retail trade, 32
Rice-cum-fish culture, 65
Rice farming, 64
Rice-fish
- area, 50, 115
- culture, 3
- germplasm, 44, 114
- production systems, 29–30, 45

Rice husks, 65
Rice plants, 20
Rural aquaculture, 21

Sadia Frontier Tract, 61
Seed
- collection, 76–77, 121
- production, 97, 129

Sewage-fed water, 17
Shifting cultivation, 61
Skilled labour, 88, 125
Small Scale Fisheries (SSF), 38
Social resources, 72
Socio-economic
- characteristics, 5, 8, 12, 26, 59, 66, 81–82
- information, 31

Stochastic frontier production model, 19
Storage facilities, 26
Structural change, 39
Subansiri river, 62
Sustainable farming practices, 31
Sustainable livelihood, 14, 22, 24

Technical efficiency, 16–17, 19
Technical inefficiency, 16
Technological change, 3
Total Revenue (TR), 86, 88, 124–25
Traditional production system, 3
Trout production, 128

Water bodies, 3–4, 23–24, 44, 62, 66, 77–78, 80, 110, 121–22
Water resource harbours, 44, 114
Water Resource Institute, 38
Water rice ecosystems, 30
Wet rice cultivation, 61
World Fish Production, 42
World Trade Organization, 28